Raisina
Chronicles

Raisina
Chronicles

India's Global Public Square

Edited by

S. Jaishankar
and Samir Saran

RUPA

Published by
Rupa Publications India Pvt. Ltd 2025
7/16, Ansari Road, Daryaganj
New Delhi 110002

Sales centres:
Bengaluru Chennai
Hyderabad Jaipur Kathmandu
Kolkata Mumbai Prayagraj

P-ISBN: 978-93-6156-508-3
E-ISBN: 978-93-6156-600-4

First impression 2025

10 9 8 7 6 5 4 3 2 1

Contents

Section 1
Changing Realities: Shifts in the World Order

Section 2
Shared Visions: Unbreakable Bilateral Ties

Section 3
New Opportunities: European Future
in the Indo-Pacific

Section 4
Guards of Honour: Forging a More Secure World

Section 5
Viral World: Outbreaks, Outliers and
Out of Control

Section 6
Unblurred Vision: Development with a Difference

Section 7
At the Helm of Power: India, Raisina and the New Way Forward

Kyriakos Mitsotakis

Prime Minister of Greece

Foreword

India and Greece discovered democracy, and each other, aeons ago. In the twenty-first century, they are discovering each other again—this time as pillars of the liberal international order. My visit to India for the Raisina Dialogue, as it enters its tenth year, is meant to emphasize the possibilities inherent in our shared vision for the world.

Our two countries have long been the source of ideas that have taken the world by storm. We have achieved this because we both believe in the virtues of discussion and debate. We recognize that without such debate the search for truth is meaningless.

Today's world is increasingly divided—between the West and the East, between the South and the North. India stands at the intersection of these divisions. Divisions can be managed, or even tempered, by open discussion. The world needs a new agora, where ideas can be tested against each other. The Raisina Dialogue, and indeed India, is an answer to that need.

A divided world needs more tangible, physical connections as well. The integration of our two seas—the Indo–Pacific and the Mediterranean—was first achieved in antiquity and can be achieved again. We can and will be partners in this endeavour—one that will benefit not just us but also our neighbours.

Greece is a nation of philosophers and explorers, and so is India. Our two peoples have much to learn from each other, and much to teach the world. And it will all begin with a commitment to the public square and to open discussion.

S. Jaishankar and Samir Saran

Minister of External Affairs of India
President, Observer Research Foundation (ORF)

Editors' Note

The Raisina Dialogue has become a feature today in the calendars of leaders around the world. It is a must-attend for all who seek to move the needle, disrupt the status quo, defend their beliefs, and create what shall be. India's flagship conference on geopolitics and geoeconomics enters its tenth year. In that time, it has emerged as a global, inclusive and wide-band forum of international importance, transcending borders and ideologies, ages and agendas, hashtags and echo chambers. It is India's 'global public square'—located in New Delhi, incubated by the world. Its purpose is to preserve and promote the often-challenged art of dialogue and working through differences. In keeping with Indian Prime Minister Shri Narendra Modi's vision of delivering public goods for the benefit of all humanity, it is indeed a platform that serves this planet.

Raisina has been crucial in propelling discourse, nurturing collaboration, and fostering a sense of shared responsibility. It is a venue for celebrating diversity in all its shapes and forms: of thought, of approaches, of beliefs, of politics. It has captured the age-old Indian premise that within us all lies a desire and power to do good. Each view must be heard, and each suggestion must be considered. Pluralism, confabulation and heterogeneity are what make us resilient and anti-fragile, and what drive the evolution of individuals and societies. This is India's own story as well: an enormous diversity that rests on a powerful timeless unity. For this reason, Raisina provides a rare opportunity for leaders and diplomats, scholars and policymakers, journalists and academics, teenagers and seasoned thinkers, business folks and civil society, all to come together to debate, deliberate, disagree and discover shared futures and common pathways.

On this occasion, we celebrate the Raisina Decade: a period during which the Dialogue has helped build regional partnerships and transcontinental collaborations while responding to global challenges. For three days every year, it has brought a fractured and polarized world together. This volume chronicles this journey and reflects on its unique strengths and attributes. And this is best done by bringing together how it is perceived by eminent participants from different parts of the world. These are the thoughts of those who have themselves experienced Raisina and contributed ideas, who have listened and spoken there, and who appreciate the difference it has made.

THE MAKING OF RAISINA

The imperative of dialogue in polarized times is self-evident. And it has gained salience precisely because the promise of globalization has been visibly broken. Most have lost faith in the once-inviting prospect of a world where different customs and cultures are welcomed, where different perspectives are appreciated, and where different interests are accepted. This came about because a few were able to ultimately control the process of globalization at the expense of the many. Global realities were recast in the image of these narrow circles to suit their interests and needs. What was meant to usher in a brave new world—more diverse and inclusive than the one before— became instead an instrument for manufacturing consent.

This has prompted multiple pushbacks. Some intellectual and others political. Its cumulative result is apparent to all today when we see how the global landscape has fragmented.

The flipside of the predicament is the extraordinary concentrations of manufacturing technology and capabilities that emerged to partner these interests. With the passage of time, every aspect of this new dominance is being leveraged. So, it should not come as a surprise that global conversations have also felt its impact. Hierarchies and architectures that had receded with history have resurfaced. And along with them, a different form of discourse and messaging.

The influence on mindsets has also been profound. Anxieties about the quality of life and the reliability of supply chains have made many societies look inward. Domestic priorities understandably prevail over international cooperation; individual interests supersede collective endeavours. Meanwhile, the guardians of the international order and the established multilateral frameworks repeat outdated mantras that lack credibility. The truth is that the self-appointed custodians of the world today are divorced from its continuance. These original architects have also lost the wherewithal to convene all stakeholders and shapers. It was therefore important for new protagonists to step in, contribute and gather. This is why India, under the leadership of its Prime Minister, felt it necessary to invest in a global arena for ideation and deliberation. At the Raisina Dialogue, panels are hosted by leaders in politics, business, media and civil society. Heads of state and foreign ministers sit next to aspiring engineers and business studies graduates. It is a space where the East and the West, the North and the South, and countless regional competitors can—and do—share a stage. Patience is prioritized over polemic, understanding over assertion, and balance over subjectivity. It is a truly global public square with an Indian postal code.

OFFERING AN INDIA WAY

This year, while the world gathers in India for Raisina Dialogue 2024, the relevance of *vasudhaiva kutumbakam* ('the world is one family') is increasingly evident. In today's fractured world, this mantra is a sorely needed acknowledgement of the inherent unity of humankind and the impact we have on each other. In this context, the India Story resonates in many corners of the globe because of the similarity of problems and the viability of solutions. The deep and persistent development challenges India is addressing offer a template of action for others to adopt and adapt. It is incumbent on India to be generous with sharing its journey, its experiences and learning, and its struggles and solutions.

Through its G20 presidency, India shared with the world a credible synthesis of nationalism and internationalism. This was based on the conviction that a major nation which effectively addresses the needs of its people can only serve humankind better. Certainly, that has been the case with India, whether we think of it as a First Responder, a Pharmacy of the World, an example of Digital Delivery, a source of trusted talent or as an innovator, a manufacturer and a supply chain link. In each case, the progress at home was reflected in greater contributions abroad. By ascending the global economic hierarchy with a view to emerging third by 2028, India is not only transforming the most populous society but also becoming an additional engine of global growth. This is much needed in an era of fairer re-globalization that is more focused on strategic autonomy. And the challenge of harmonizing the local with the global is one that is addressed by drawing on India's own heritage and outlook.

The Raisina Dialogue reflects the conviction that our

journeys must be open to all. It advocates an open architecture for governance, policy, and storytelling. Every success and failure, every experience and innovation, has relevance for someone somewhere in the world. Raisina is a platform for such discourse, mirroring the innate pluralism of India. Consequently, its annual gathering is a meeting ground for a great variety of people, perspectives and topics.

WHY BHARAT MATTERS

The change that we have witnessed in the last decade has not just been a quantitative expansion. This transformation has been one equally of thought processes, self-confidence and self-reliance. It draws on generations of heritage and culture, thereby creating greater self-awareness about our identity. There is a greater seriousness, too, in realizing visions and achieving goals. Not least, there is a clear sense of what we were and are, which is essential to deciding where we want to go. Mediating effectively between tradition and technology has always been key to the quest for modernity. Today, the ability to delineate our own path and expand our decisional space is characteristic of our progress. The combination of all of these has helped to make India much more Bharat.

Confronted with an uncertain world, this means drawing on our own experiences and arriving at our judgements in the search for solutions. Conflicting pulls and pressures will press us to take positions that may not always be in our best interest. They could be presented as global norms or natural choices. It is here that independent thinking arrived at through detailed discourse can make a difference. When it came to the Indo–Pacific, we embraced a strategic concept that is clearly to our benefit. And joined a mechanism that promoted both global good and national interest.

That such steps were a departure from the past was not a discouragement. Similarly, when it came to the Ukraine conflict, we articulated the concerns of a large part of the world on its economic consequences. By contesting a narrative that served a particular region, we were also able to soften the impact on our own people. Bharat means having the courage to be contrary when needed, contributive when required, and confident at all times.

Raisina is the venue where such conversations happen. It is the living, dynamic bridge where the world comes to understand us, and where we communicate with the world. Raisina is the vehicle for this dialogue, where the world absorbs Bharat and Bharat in turn shapes the world.

THE RAISINA DIALECTIC

The Raisina Dialogue stands out currently as a broad-based forum that engages freely in debate, discussion and disputation. The coming together of diverse perspectives in a productive collision often results in new insights and solutions. There are particular reasons for the energy and effervescence that characterizes its activities. They emanate from its interdisciplinary nature, inclusive participation, equitable agenda and democratic ethos.

Raisina is designed to reap the dividends that flow from the interactions of different disciplines and methods of thinking. Such cross-sectoral discourse is of utmost importance for breaking down silos and enhancing understanding. Diplomats must speak to scholars and academics, while international relations thinkers should engage business leaders. It is common to see leaders in politics, business, media and civil society share a stage for discussion. Rigid policy conversations are shaken up with the introduction of freer scholarly interventions. This holistic approach makes discussions more complete, more comprehensive, and ultimately more effective.

Inclusiveness is at the heart of the Raisina spirit. The Dialogue welcomes views from across the globe that have not found space in traditional and established arenas. It allows conversations of a different kind because the voices themselves are different: they are younger; they are more diverse; they are from geographies that are often ignored or from institutions which cannot break into the international pecking order. They are more representative of the way the world actually looks. As a result, Raisina becomes a place for discovering new talent, new ideas, new perspectives, and new people. It acts as a springboard, a gateway, an all-access pass for these new protagonists and narratives to be allowed entry into the traditional forums.

Concerns of equity and fairness pervade the choice of topics for the panel discussions. Most international forums concern themselves with the first billion people of the world. Raisina is that exception where discussions focus on the interests of the next seven billion. Matters of food security are given as much prominence as the battles between tech platforms. Questions of regional development, energy access, public goods and employment are as important as concerns of war and peace, anti-trust regulation, and the quest for the ideal liberal society. Past empires are now talking back and demanding their place at the table. The Global South has been noticeable in that regard, be it in its self-perception or self-confidence. Raisina reflects this reality because it has consciously moved beyond privilege. It is not merely an active gathering but also a very contemporary one.

As a dialogue that is greater than the sum of its parts, its conversations take place not merely during the three days of the conference but also in the periods before and after. It is a zone where ideas are incubated, where solutions are assessed and reassessed, and where visions clash, compete, contest and cooperate. New sentiments are articulated, and outdated perspectives discarded. Discussions are frank and usually honest; they could be provocative but are always constructive. Through its reputation and impact, this approach is now becoming the new normal.

A DECADE OF DIALOGUE

As the Raisina Dialogue enters its tenth year, it is fair to say that we have come a great distance. What started as a hundred people in a room has become India's premier conference and a forum of international note. The Dialogue has captured the global imagination precisely because it happens to be in a New India.

The success of Raisina has also been driven by the support, leadership and commitment of the Indian government. The Prime Minister himself has made it a point to be present at each inaugural session of the Dialogue since its second edition in 2017, and has delivered an address once in person and once virtually. By attending the Dialogue but foregoing the microphone, the Prime Minister has reminded the world that, many times, to listen is more important than to speak. He has elevated the act of being in a Raisina audience to learning from other experiences, grappling with other perspectives, and absorbing the vantage points that others have brought. He has personally demolished the hierarchy between the speaking class on the one hand and the audience members on the other. Raisina is as much about being a listener as it is about being a speaker. It is a reminder that every idea demands careful consideration—that debate is the food for life itself. Here, difference is never shunned because it is the basis of working harder to come together.

To commemorate a decade of dialogue, this volume brings together essays written by eminent voices from across the world as well as speeches delivered at Raisina by world leaders and heads of states.

Raisina Chronicles opens with a foreword by *Kyriakos Mitsotakis,* the Prime Minister of Greece. Greece and India, both ancient cradles of democracy, are discovering each other again in the twenty-first century. Mr Mitsotakis advocates for open discussion as a means to bridge global divisions, proposing the integration of the Indo–Pacific and the Mediterranean as a path towards greater global unity and cooperation.

In her essay, *Mette Frederiksen,* the Prime Minister of Denmark, discusses the interconnected crises facing the planet, encompassing climate, environment, health and military conflicts. In such a world, the India–Denmark Green Strategic Partnership exemplifies successful collaboration, addressing climate goals and creating a model for global impact. She stresses the importance of global cooperation and reinvigorating our commitment to tackle shared challenges. In the next piece, *Tanja Fajon,* the Deputy Prime Minister of Slovenia, reflects on the 2023 Raisina Dialogue, praising its diverse discussions on global challenges. She discusses the urgent need for international cooperation, advocating effective multilateralism and UN reform. Lauding the inclusion of youth and women in Raisina discussions, she expresses optimism about India–Slovenia cooperation.

Penny Wong, the Australian Minister of Foreign Affairs, stresses the importance of forums like Raisina for strategic thinking amidst escalating security challenges. She underscores Australia's partnership with India, citing shared history and the Comprehensive Strategic Partnership, praising collaborative efforts in economic, climate and educational initiatives.

In his essay, *Prince Faisal bin Farhan Al Saud*, the Minister of Foreign Affairs in Saudi Arabia, writes about the deep-rooted cultural ties between India and the Arab world which have now evolved into a robust strategic partnership. Trade relations have flourished, with India being the Kingdom's second-largest trading partner. He is confident that the Saudi–Indian partnership promises a prosperous future for both nations. *Kwame Owino*, the CEO of the Institute of Economic Affairs, and *Jackline Kagume*, the Constitution, Law and Economy Programme head at IEA, emphasize the African Union's (AU) admission to the G20 as a significant step for global economic governance. They highlight the AU's potential for pushing for global institution reforms in an effort to counteract the trend of de-globalization.

The Chairman of the Japan Bank for International Cooperation, *Tadashi Maeda* touches upon India's economic growth, its partnership with Japan, and the significance of the Indo–Pacific region. He stresses enhanced India–Japan cooperation amidst global challenges. *Admiral Sir Antony Radakin*, the Chief of the Defence Staff of the United Kingdom (UK), explores the changing dynamics between the UK and India in the 2020s and highlights the UK's interest in the Indo–Pacific towards expanding partnerships in maritime, air and land security, as well as promoting defence collaboration with India.

Nitya Mohan Khemka, the director of PATH and a lecturer at the University of Cambridge, advocates for targeted strategies to increase the representation of women in leadership, highlighting the systematic barriers and biases women face in entering senior finance roles. She concludes that women leading development banks is not just about gender equality but also crucial for efficient and effective development financing. *Camila dos Santos*, the International Relations Advisor at Rio de Janeiro City Hall, discusses the crucial role of addressing gender inequality at the G20 summit, paying particular attention to the disproportionate burden of unpaid domestic and caregiving work borne by women, especially those from marginalized groups. The imperative for comprehensive public policies in support of caregiving is foregrounded.

Admiral John Aquilino, the Commander of the United States Indo–Pacific Command, reflects on the significant impact of the Raisina Dialogue in shaping multilateral engagements, particularly in advancing the US–India relationship. According to him, Raisina has played a crucial role in fostering collaboration, leading to milestones such as the Quad's revival and defence agreements between the two nations.

A Raisina regular, *General Angus Campbell*, the Chief of the Defence Force of Australia, and *Greg Moriarty*, the Secretary of the Department of Defence of Australia, emphasize the deepening defence and security partnership between India and Australia and highlight India's pivotal role in Australia's strategic vision for the Indo–Pacific. *General Koji Yamazaki*, the former Chief of the Joint Staff of the Japan Self-Defense Force, praises the Raisina Dialogue for its role as an 'ideas arena' and emphasizes the deepening Japan–India defence cooperation with the end of a Free and Open Indo–Pacific.

In their piece, *Rosa Balfour* and *Zakaria Al Shmaly*, director and research analyst, respectively, at Carnegie Europe, argue that the European Union's foreign policy reflects double standards, that the Global South's perception of the EU stands in contrast to the EU's self-perception, and also that the EU needs to reform policies to improve its engagement with the Global South. *Anirban Sarma*, deputy director at Observer Research Foundation, makes the case that India has, over its G20 presidency, raised a significant level of awareness about digital public infrastructure (DPI) and its transformative potential for facilitating financial inclusion and tech-enabled development. He argues that India's DPI model, the India Stack, has revolutionized public service delivery and serves as a framework whose appeal transcends the Global South.

Amrita Narlikar, president and professor at the German Institute for Global and Area Studies, argues for preserving globalization by fundamentally rethinking its direction and scale, highlighting its benefits and inherent problems. She critiques the current model's security, sustainability and ownership deficits, and proposes 'the Bharat Way' as a path towards a more secure, inclusive and sustainable globalization.

Carl Bildt, the former Prime Minister of Sweden, addresses geopolitical tensions, emphasizes the need for global trade agreements, and explores the impact of new technologies, climate change, and global health challenges. He highlights India's influential role in global discourse, with the Raisina Dialogue serving as a vital platform for fostering diverse perspectives on pressing issues. *Scott Morrison,* the former Prime Minister of Australia, refers to the enduring friendship between Australia and India. Reflecting on the Raisina Dialogue, he underscores the importance of appreciating India's perspective and aligning Western strategic outlooks with India's role as a leader in the Global South. *Marcelo Ebrard,* the former Secretary of Foreign Affairs of Mexico, shares thoughts on the growing importance of the Asia–Pacific region, particularly India, with whom Mexico has strengthened diplomatic relations over 70 years. He praises the Raisina Dialogue for addressing global challenges and promoting dialogue, inclusion and lasting solutions.

Mohammed Soliman, Director of the Strategic Technologies and Cyber Security Program at the Middle East Institute, analyses the Middle East's complex dynamics, juxtaposing the ongoing Israel–Gaza conflict with the stability offered by the Abraham Accords and other minilateral formats. *David Petraeus*, the former Director of the Central Intelligence Agency, looks at Raisina as a metaphor for India. He argues that the dialogue encapsulates India's complex stance, embracing both Quad and BRICS affiliations, reflecting its unique role and evolving identity. As India grows in influence, the Raisina Dialogue becomes an increasingly important global gathering.

And finally, concluding the Raisina Chronicles is the former Prime Minister of Canada, *Stephen J. Harper*, with an essay titled 'India Takes Its Rightful Place in an Evolving Global Order'. Mr Harper highlights India's significant global role, emphasizing its influence on Indo–Pacific stability, SDG progress, global democracy, and climate change. He commends the Raisina Dialogue as a vital platform showcasing India's confidence and significance in an evolving world order.

The Raisina Chronicles is not just a compilation of contributions from eminent leaders to mark a decade of dialoguing at Raisina Hill; it is also a report card of a decade of world affairs. The original essays and selected addresses delivered at the Dialogue and included in this publication collectively offer some crucial insights.

First, that a dialogue out of India matters because it brings a unique capability and commitment to the imperative of discussions and deliberations. Second, Raisina's journey is a reflection of Bharat's emergence. And as its engagement with the world evolves, we, at the Dialogue, will have to continue to innovate and upgrade. Finally, now that the Dialogue is a global good in the assessment of many, it will have to enter the second decade of its existence more aware of its wider responsibility.

Section 1

Changing Realities: Shifts in the World Order

Narendra Modi

Prime Minister of India

The New Normal: Multilateralism with Multipolarity

TODAY SEEMS TO BE A DAY OF SPEECHES. JUST A WHILE ago, we heard President Xi and Prime Minister May. Here I am with my words. Perhaps an overdose for some. Or a problem of plenty for 24/7 news channels.

It is a great privilege to speak to you at the inauguration of the second edition of the Raisina Dialogue. Excellency Karzai, Prime Minister Harper, Prime Minister Kevin Rudd, it is a pleasure to see you in Delhi. Also, a warm welcome to all the guests. Over the next couple of days, you would hold numerous conversations on the state of the world around us. You would debate its certainty and prevailing flux, its conflicts and risks, its successes and opportunities, its past behaviours and likely prognosis, and its potential black swans and the new normal.

Friends, in May 2014, the people of India also ushered in a new normal. My fellow Indians spoke in one voice to entrust my government with a mandate for change. Change not just of attitudes but of mindsets. Change from a state of drift to one of purposeful action. Change to take bold decisions. A mandate in which reform would not be enough unless it transforms our economy and society. A transformation that is embedded in the aspiration and optimism of India's youth, and in the boundless energy of its millions. Every day at work, I draw on this sacred energy. Every day at work, my 'to do list' is guided by the constant drive to reform and transform India, for prosperity and security of all Indians. Friends, I am aware that India's transformation is not separated from its external context. Our economic growth; the welfare of our farmers; the employment opportunities for our youth; our access to capital, technology, markets and resources; and the security of our nation: all of them are deeply impacted by developments in the world. But the reverse is also true.

The world needs India's sustained rise as much as India needs the world. Our desire to change our country has an indivisible link with the external world. It is, therefore, only natural that India's choices at home and our international priorities form part of a seamless continuum, firmly anchored in India's transformational goals.

Friends, India is pursuing its transformation in unsettled times, which is equally the result of human progress and violent turmoil. For multiple reasons and at multiple levels, the world is going through profound changes. Globally connected societies, digital opportunities, technology shifts, knowledge boom and innovation are leading the march of humanity. But sluggish growth and economic volatility are also a sobering fact. Physical borders may be less relevant in this age of bits and bytes. But walls within nations, a sentiment against trade and migration, and rising parochial and protectionist attitudes across the globe are also in stark evidence. The result: globalization gains are at risk and economic gains are no longer easy to come by. Instability, violence, extremism, exclusion and transnational threats continue to proliferate in dangerous directions. And non-state actors are significant contributors to the spread of such challenges. Institutions and architectures built for a different world, by a different world, are outdated. Posing a barrier to effective multilateralism. As the world begins to re-order itself a quarter century after the strategic clarity of the Cold War, the dust has not yet settled on what has replaced it. But a couple of things are clear. Political and military power is diffused and distributed.

The multipolarity of the world, and an increasingly multipolar Asia, is a dominant fact today. And we welcome it. Because it captures the reality of the rise of many nations. It accepts that voices of many, not views of a few, should shape the global agenda. Therefore, we need to guard against any instinct or inclination that promotes exclusion, especially in Asia. The focus of this conference on 'Multilateralism with Multipolarity' is thus timely.

Friends, we inhabit a strategically complex environment. In the broad sweep of history, the changing world is not necessarily a new situation. The crucial question is how nations should act in a situation where the frames of reference are shifting rapidly. Our choices and actions are based on the strength of our national power.

Our strategic intent is shaped by our civilizational ethos of यथार्थवाद (realism), सह–अस्तित्व (co-existence), सहयोग (cooperation) and सहभागित (partnership). This finds expression in a clear and responsible articulation of our national interests.

The prosperity of Indians, both at home and abroad, and the security of our citizens are of paramount importance. But self-interest alone is neither in our culture nor in our behaviour. Our actions and aspirations, capacities and human capital, democracy and demography, and strength and success, will continue to be an anchor for all-round regional and global progress. Our economic and political rise represents a regional and global opportunity of great significance. It is a force for peace, a factor for stability, and an engine for regional and global prosperity.

For my government, this has meant a path of international engagement focused on:

- Rebuilding connectivity, restoring bridges, and rejoining India with our immediate and extended geographies.
- Shaping relationships networked with India's economic priorities.
- Making India a human resource power to be reckoned with by connecting our talented youth to global needs and opportunities.
- Building development partnerships that extend from the islands of the Indian Ocean and the Pacific Ocean to the islands of the Caribbean and from the great continent of Africa to the Americas.
- Creating Indian narratives on global challenges.
- Helping reconfigure, reinvigorate and rebuild global institutions and organizations.
- Spreading the benefits of India's civilizational legacies, including yoga and Ayurveda, as a global good. Transformation, therefore, is not just a domestic focus. It encompasses our global agenda.

For me, '*sab ka saath, sab ka vikas*' is not just a vision for India. It is a belief for the whole world. And it manifests itself in several layers, multiple themes and different geographies.

Let me turn to those that are closest to us in terms of geography and shared interests. We have seen a major shift towards our neighbours captured in our determined 'neighbourhood-first' approach. The people of South Asia are joined by blood, shared history, culture and aspirations. The optimism of its youth seeks change, opportunities, progress and prosperity. A thriving, well-connected and integrated neighbourhood is my dream. In the last two-and-a-half years, we have partnered with almost all our neighbours to bring the region together. Where necessary, we have shed the burdens of our past for the progressive future of our region. The result of our efforts is there to see.

In Afghanistan, despite distance and difficulties in transit, our partnership assists in reconstruction by building institutions and capacities. In the backdrop, our security engagement has deepened. The completion of Afghanistan's parliament building and the India-Afghanistan Friendship Dam are two shining examples of our dedication to forge developmental partnerships.

With Bangladesh, we have achieved greater convergence and political understanding through connectivity, infrastructure projects and, significantly, the settlement of the land and maritime boundaries.

In Nepal, Sri Lanka, Bhutan and the Maldives, our overall engagement in infrastructure, connectivity, energy and development projects is a source of progress and stability in the region.

My vision for our neighbourhood puts a premium on peaceful and harmonious ties with the entire South Asia. That vision had led me to invite leaders of all SAARC nations, including Pakistan, for my swearing-in. For this vision, I had also travelled to Lahore. But India alone cannot walk the path of peace. It also has to be Pakistan's journey to make. Pakistan must walk away from terror if it wants to walk towards dialogue with India.

Ladies and gentlemen, further west, we have redefined, in a short span of time and despite uncertainty and conflict, our partnerships with the Gulf and West Asia, including Saudi Arabia, UAE, Qatar, and Iran. Next week, I will have the pleasure to host His Highness the Crown Prince of Abu Dhabi as the chief guest at India's Republic Day. We have not just focused on changing the perception. We have also changed the reality of our ties. This has helped us protect and promote our security interests, nurture strong economic and energy ties, and advance the material and social welfare of around eight million Indians.

In Central Asia, too, we have built our ties on the edifice of shared history and culture to unlock new vistas of prosperous partnerships. Our membership of the Shanghai Cooperation Organisation provides a strong institutional link to our engagement with Central Asian nations. We have invested in the all-round prosperity of our Central Asian brothers and sisters and have brought about a successful reset to long-standing relationships in that region.

To our east, our engagement with Southeast Asia is at the centre of our Act East Policy. We have built a close engagement with the institutional structures in the region such as the East Asia Summit. Our partnership with ASEAN and its member countries has served to enhance commerce, technology, investment, development and security partnerships in the region. It has also advanced our broad strategic interests and stability in the region. In our engagement with China, as President Xi and I agreed, we have sought to tap the vast area of commercial and business opportunities in the relationship. I see the development of India and China as an unprecedented opportunity, for our two countries and for the whole world. At the same time, it is not unnatural for two large neighbouring powers to have some differences. In the management of our relationship, and for peace and progress in the region, both our countries need to show sensitivity and respect for each other's concerns and interests.

Friends, the prevailing wisdom tells us that this century belongs to Asia. The sharpest trajectory of change is happening in Asia. There are large and vibrant pools of progress and prosperity that spread across the landscape of this region. But rising ambition and rivalries are generating visible stress points. The steady increase in military power, resources, and wealth in the Asia-Pacific has raised the stakes for its security. Therefore, the security architecture in the region must be open, transparent, balanced and inclusive. And promote dialogue and predictable behaviour rooted in international norms and respect for sovereignty.

Friends, over the past two-and-a-half years, we have given a strong momentum to our engagement with the United States, Russia, Japan and other major global powers. With them, we not only share a desire to cooperate, we also hold converging views on opportunities and challenges that face us. These partnerships are a good fit with India's economic priorities and defence and security. With the United States, our actions have brought speed, substance and strength to the entire spectrum of our engagement. In my conversation with President-elect Donald Trump, we agreed to keep building on these gains in our strategic partnership. Russia is an abiding friend. President Putin and I have held long conversations on the challenges that confront the world today. Our trusted and strategic partnership, especially in the field of defence, has deepened. Our investments in new drivers of our relationship and the emphasis on energy, trade and S&T linkages are showing successful results.

We also enjoy a truly strategic partnership with Japan, whose contours now stretch to all fields of economic activity. Prime Minister Abe and I have spoken of our determination to intensify our cooperation further. With Europe, we have a vision of strong partnership in India's development, especially in knowledge industry and smart urbanization.

Friends, India has, for decades, been at the forefront of sharing our capacities and strengths with fellow developing countries. With our brothers and sisters in Africa, we have further strengthened our ties in the last couple of years and built meaningful development partnerships on the solid foundation of decades of traditional friendship and historical links. Today the footprint of our development partnership stretches all across the globe.

Ladies and gentlemen, India has a long history of being a maritime nation. In all directions, our maritime interests are strategic and significant. The arc of influence of the Indian Ocean extends well beyond its littoral limits. Our initiative of SAGAR—Security and Growth for All in the Region—is not just limited to safeguarding our mainland and islands. It defines our efforts to deepen economic and security cooperation in our maritime relationships. We know that convergence, cooperation and collective action will advance economic activity and peace in our maritime region. We also believe that the primary responsibility for peace, prosperity and security in the Indian Ocean rests with those who live in this region. Ours is not an exclusive approach. And we aim to bring countries together on the basis of respect for international law. We believe that respecting the freedom of navigation and adhering to international norms are essential for peace and economic growth in the larger and interlinked marine geography of the Indo-Pacific.

Friends, we appreciate the compelling logic of regional connectivity for peace, progress and prosperity. In our choices and through our actions, we have sought to overcome barriers to our outreach to West and Central Asia, and eastwards to the Asia-Pacific. Two clear and successful examples of this are the tripartite agreement with Iran and Afghanistan on Chabahar and our commitment to bring on line the International North-South Transport Corridor. However, equally, connectivity in itself cannot override or undermine the sovereignty of other nations. Only by respecting the sovereignty of countries involved can regional connectivity corridors fulfil their promise and avoid differences and discord.

Friends, true to our traditions, we have shouldered the international burden of our commitments. We have led assistance and relief efforts in times of disaster. We were a credible first responder during the earthquake in Nepal, the evacuation from Yemen, and during humanitarian crises in the Maldives and Fiji. We have also not hesitated in shouldering our responsibility for the maintenance of international peace and security. We have increased collaboration on coastal surveillance, white shipping information, and fighting non-traditional threats like piracy, smuggling and organized crime. We have also shaped alternative narratives on long-standing global challenges. Our strong belief in delinking terrorism from religion and rejecting artificial distinctions between good and bad terrorism are now a global talking point. And those in our neighbourhood who support violence, encourage hatred and export terror stand isolated and ignored.

On the other pressing challenge of global warming, we have moved into a leading role. We have an ambitious agenda and an equally aggressive target to generate 175 gigawatts from renewable energy. And we have already made a good start. We have shared our civilizational traditions to promote harmonious living with nature. We also brought the international community together to create an International Solar Alliance, to harness the energy of the sun to propel human growth. A high point of our efforts has been the revival of international interest in the cultural and spiritual richness of India's civilizational stream. Today, Buddhism, yoga, and Ayurveda are recognized as the invaluable heritage of humanity as a whole. India will celebrate this common heritage every step of the way. As it builds bridges across countries and regions and promotes overall well-being.

Ladies and gentlemen, in conclusion, let me say this. In connecting with the world, our ancient scriptures have guided us. The Rig Veda says आ नो भद्रो: क्रत्वो यन्तु विश्वत ('let noble thoughts come to me from all directions').

As a society, we have always favoured the needs of many over the want of one. And preferred partnerships over polarization. We hold the belief that success of one must propel the growth of many. Our task is cut out. And our vision is clear. Our journey of transformation begins at home. And is strongly supported through our constructive and collaborative partnerships that span the globe. With resolute steps at home and an expanding network of reliable friendships abroad, we will grasp the promise of a future that belongs to over a billion Indians. And in this endeavour, you will find in India, my friends, a beacon of peace and progress, stability and success, and access and accommodation.

Thank you. Thank you very much.

This speech was delivered at the inaugural address at the 2nd Raisina Dialogue, 2017 (17 January 2017).

António Guterres

Secretary-General, United Nations

The New Normal: Multilateralism with Multipolarity

THANK YOU TO THE OBSERVER RESEARCH FOUNDATION and the Indian Ministry of External Affairs for this invitation.

Foreign Secretary Jaishankar and I spoke last month about multilateralism with multipolarity, the theme of the Dialogue. Today's conflicts are more complex and interlinked, human rights violations are occurring on a mass scale, and terrorism affects every region. The rule-based international order is under threat.

We have a multipolar environment, but we need multilateral solutions. And the United Nations is the cornerstone of multilateralism.

It is no longer enough to address crisis situations. People and countries pay too high a price if we only deal with conflicts. And that is why I am calling for a surge in diplomacy for peace.

Now, the causes of crisis are interlinked. And, to respond, the UN has to connect its efforts for peace and security, for sustainable developments, and for human rights. We have the plans: the 2030 Agenda for sustainable development along with the resolutions on sustaining peace. But now we need an integrated approach and changes in our culture, strategy, structures and operations. I am committed to achieving a shift from putting out fires to preventing, and sustaining peace. Partnerships with regional organizations are essential.

The Raisina Dialogue can contribute to preventive diplomacy in Asia. Asia is one of the most diverse regions in the world. India itself is very diverse. The Indian Constitution recognizes 22 official languages and India has people practising all major religions. Diversity is a strength. But we see tensions in Asia, often along communal, societal, or religious lines.

You speak in the theme of the Dialogue about navigating Asia's new normal. The way to navigate, in Asia and globally, is based on common values: peace, justice, respect, human rights, tolerance, and solidarity.

Our challenge is to build trust in each other and in institutions, including the United Nations. And I'm committed to inspiring trust in the UN. I hope you will join me in working to making 2017 a year of peace.

This speech was delivered at the inaugural session of the 2nd Raisina Dialogue, 2017 (17 January 2017).

Erna Solberg

Prime Minister of Norway

A World Reorder: New Geometrics, Fluid Partnerships, Uncertain Outcomes

THE TIES BETWEEN INDIA AND NORWAY GO BACK hundreds of years. The first possible evidence we have of links between Norway and India dates back to the year 834, from a Viking ship discovered by accident by a farmer in 1903 in a burial mound in Norway. The bodies of two women were found in the ship. Buried with them, archaeologists found items that were meant to accompany them to the afterlife. These included fine silks and a small Buddha-like figure decorated with four golden swastikas. These items may have originated from the Indian subcontinent, although we will never know for sure.

In any case, they came to Norway by sea. The oceans were as essential to our Viking ancestors as they are to us today. They are a vital part of both our history and our future. As the world population continues to grow, more and more people will depend on the oceans for development and prosperity.

By the middle of this century, the world population is expected to increase to ten billion people. This means that we must look to the oceans in order to ensure sufficient food, jobs, energy and economic growth. But this will only be possible if ocean resources are used and extracted sustainably. We all have a stake in building a sustainable blue economy.

BUILDING A BLUE ECONOMY

As leaders of maritime nations, both India and Norway know that we have a special responsibility to protect the oceans as a source of food, health and livelihoods. Ambitious new initiatives have been launched to develop India's blue economy. Prime Minister Modi has presented a vision of sustainability and growth for all people in the region.

One of the goals of my government's ocean strategy is to promote sustainable value creation and employment in the ocean-based industries. Our ambition is to facilitate the transfer of expertise and technology across industrial sectors. For instance, Norwegian technology developed for the offshore oil and gas sector is now being used in aquaculture and renewable energy installations, like offshore wind. If we are to build a sustainable ocean economy, we must stop the degradation of the world's marine ecosystems. We must improve the health of the oceans.

That is why Norway has established the High-Level Panel for a Sustainable Ocean Economy. As the only ocean policy body consisting of currently-serving world leaders, our ambition is to trigger, amplify and accelerate action to promote ocean protection and productivity. We will encourage action across the board, in policy, governance and financing. We need to move towards integrated ocean management instead of managing the ocean sector by sector. This must be based on scientific knowledge and take into account the full range of opportunities and risks.

Our goal is to advance a new contract that will both protect the oceans and optimize their value for all people. Norway looks forward to continuing its cooperation with India on this issue. Global ocean management means that we must work together to share both the benefits and the burdens. The bilateral Ocean Dialogue mechanism we have established will provide an excellent tool for this purpose.

Successful cooperation depends on a robust and predictable legal and institutional framework in the ocean space. The United Nations Convention on the Law of the Sea provides the legal framework for ocean diplomacy. India and Norway share democratic values and an emphasis on international norms and laws. The rules-based international order has served Norway well. A concrete example is the settlement of the maritime boundary dispute between Norway and Russia in 2010. Our disputed maritime claims were in areas with an abundance of natural resources. Achieving an agreement was not easy, but it was in our mutual interest. The agreement is important for our future blue economy. We commend India for respecting the rulings of the International Tribunal for the Law of the Sea on the question of disputed maritime areas.

One thing is for sure: When large countries respect international law, smaller countries take note. The principle 'might is right' cannot be used as a basis for governing our oceans, or anything else for that matter. One area where large and small countries work together under common institutions is the Arctic.

THE COMMON THREAT

Norway is an Arctic nation. Much of our territory lies north of the Arctic Circle. Sea areas account for a large part of this territory. For us, the Arctic is not a remote, icy wilderness. For many Norwegians, it is where we live, raise our families, and run our businesses. As a result of climate change, we are seeing rapid and dramatic changes to the Arctic environment. The consequences of climate change are severe, not only for the local communities in the Arctic but also for the planet as a whole.

Rising sea levels and altered climatic conditions will have a global impact. The changes are happening fast, so fast that researchers are struggling to understand and predict the effects they will eventually have on ecosystems. No country can on its own acquire the knowledge that is needed. International research cooperation is the only way forward. There is growing evidence that temperature swings in the Arctic are affecting the melting of snow in the Himalayas and the Indian monsoons.

The worrying developments in the Arctic show the interconnected nature of our global challenges. I am therefore pleased that India and Norway have enjoyed close research cooperation on the Arctic and climate change for many years. We are among only a few countries in the world to have research activities at both the North Pole and the South Pole. This cooperation is of great value to us.

The Arctic Council is the most important forum for discussing issues of common interest relating to the Arctic. India is now an observer state, along with several other Asian countries. The Arctic has become an arena for cooperation between Europe, North America and Asia. This is presenting us with new opportunities. We hope to see an even stronger Indian engagement in the work of the Arctic Council in the time ahead.

We started with the narrative about the treasures that were discovered in a Viking burial tomb. They came to Norway by sea, and they were buried with a ship believed to be needed in the afterlife. This story reflects our shared dependence on the oceans. But it also highlights the importance of international trade, long before globalization. Global trade has led to increased prosperity for many. Extreme poverty has been halved, people live longer, child mortality rates are falling, and more girls attend school than ever before. Global political cooperation, global trade, and international law have been crucial to this progress. But we also have to recognize that globalization has not been equally beneficial for all.

Many people feel left out by globalization. This is a very real challenge. Exclusion can spur radicalization. It can undermine confidence in international institutions and cooperation. Eventually, it could weaken respect for international law, human rights, and even our security architecture.

To counter this exclusion, we must secure the future welfare of a rapidly growing population. Our job as leaders is to deliver security, jobs, education and healthcare. We must deliver results. We must ensure that our citizens feel the positive effects of growth and globalization. We must deal with the challenges of globalization while at the same time maximizing the benefits for our citizens. This requires both protection and reform of fundamental trade norms. We cannot afford to let protectionism, discrimination and economic rivalry define our future. Norway and India both benefit from rules-based international trade. We stand only to lose if this is undermined.

The WTO is essential for Norway and our interaction with the world. I believe rules-based trade is just as important for our partners. Free trade creates winners. Protectionism does not. In order to benefit all, rights, rules and responsibilities must be modernized to fit our current global economy. This is vital if we are to build a world where people's potential, creativity and hopes for the future can be realized through cooperation, knowledge exchange, and trade.

A GLOBAL RESPONSE

The consequences of instability affect us all. Global security threats require global responses. Areas of conflict and instability are breeding grounds for violent extremism and international terrorism. Violent extremism, conflict and instability lead to humanitarian crises and violations of human rights. These, in turn, are some of the main drivers of both regular and irregular migration. Terrorism and violent extremism affect us all and are not limited to any single ideology, religion or belief. In the continued fight against violent extremism, we must apply a whole-of-society approach. We must address the root causes. Security is closely linked to sustainable development.

We must boost trade and job creation. We have to be able to build capacity for generating domestic revenue and strengthen our public service delivery. Simultaneously, we must keep coming up with innovative and modern ways to combat corruption. Corruption fuels inequality, crime, instability and violence. In the same breath, we still have a long way to go to achieve and ensure women's rights and participation. This is crucial for development and lasting peace and stability.

The international community has agreed on the Sustainable Development Goals (SDGs)—the roadmap to the future we want. We all have a stake in this. The issues concern all of us. If we succeed in reaching the SDGs, we will have done much to address many of the challenges we face today, including poverty, inequality, extremism, health issues and climate change. Since 2016, I have co-chaired the UN Secretary-General's group of SDG advocates. The 17 goals make it very clear that, in this context, we are all developing countries.

Norway has frequently been ranked as number one in the Human Development Index, but we still have a lot of work to do to achieve the SDGs. India, of course, has played an important role in shaping the SDGs. The fact that India, with its massive scale and vast resources, is devoting itself to achieving the SDGs will have a global impact. I greatly appreciate Prime Minister Modi's leadership in this arena.

We have no time to lose. Sustainable change cannot be achieved overnight. It requires hard work and we must work together. The effects of climate change, conflicts, gender violence, forced migration and pandemics do not respect borders. Working together has enabled us to do far more than we could have done alone. India and Norway share the goal of solving global challenges in cooperation rather than isolation. Norway and India share many values and a deep commitment to democracy and a rules-based world order.

We live in times of great change. From Norway's perspective, global trends have been the cause of both our prosperity and many of our challenges. Trade conflicts, geopolitical tensions, violent extremism, climate change and instability at the global level directly affect us at home. But so do the benefits of world trade, the global fight against infectious diseases, and the rule of law. And while we are seeing great changes, there are also constants. The oceans are still there with their potential to provide wealth and development. To paraphrase the great Mahatma Gandhi, there is enough for everyone's need, but not enough for everyone's greed. And the monsoon winds still blow across the Indian Ocean, as they did in Viking times.

This speech was delivered at the inaugural address at the 4th Raisina Dialogue, 2019 (8 January 2019).

Carl Bildt

Former Prime Minister of Sweden

Navigating Fissures in an Evolving Global Landscape

IT WAS ONLY IN 2016 THAT THE FIRST RAISINA DIALOGUE was held, but in the short time since then, it has already established itself as one of the premier global forums on issues of geopolitics, geoeconomics and geotechnology. One of the reasons for this is undoubtedly the increasing weight of India's voice in the global discourse, as it is the world's most populous nation and largest democracy. India's skilful handling of the G20 presidency in 2023 reinforced its centrality on the global stage. But as important as this is, I believe the main reason for the rise of the Raisina Dialogue is that it has managed to attract a broader array of voices from a wider part of the world than perhaps any other international gathering that it could be compared with.

GLOBAL TUMULT

The times we live in are challenging, characterized by the simultaneous rise of geopolitical tensions that divide the world and global challenges that demand a more cohesive response from the international community. While there is a pressing need to achieve more by collective action, our ability to do so is increasingly endangered. The fissures from ongoing geopolitical tensions are obvious. In Europe, Russia has launched a large-scale aggression with the explicit aim of depriving Ukraine of the right to choose its future and subsuming it within some new version of a Greater Russian Empire. In Asia, a more assertive China is building up its military might, expecting other countries to bow to its will. And with the United States seeing its position of military supremacy under threat, moves and countermoves inevitably lead to an increase in tensions.

The shifting power balances in a world which is now multipolar has inflicted challenges upon existing multinational institutions and structures, opening up the scope for new conflicts to emerge. We have seen the Palestine issue re-emerge with a vengeance, putting into question many assumptions about where that important region is heading. Meanwhile, the issue of Afghanistan has disappeared from the headlines, but whether that will remain the case, or if that issue will also return with a vengeance, is another of the many open questions we are facing in the days to come. The rise of geopolitical tensions has also endangered a collective response towards sustaining peace and stability. The United Nations Security Council (UNSC) still sits as a dated reflection of 1945 while facing paralysis in delivering functional resolutions to one crisis after another, all due to disagreements among its permanent members. The capture of the Council by the political interests of some permanent members has arrested the efficacy of the global institutional architecture to deliver and maintain solutions to conflicts that have the potential to destabilize crucial regions. The disastrous conflict in West Asia has compounded the perception of our institutions as suboptimal for defusing geopolitical fault lines.

Geoeconomics has also made its comeback on the global scene. The spectacular economic rise of China during the last few decades has changed the global economy to a large extent. Even in times of mounting economic difficulties, nearly a third of total growth in the global economy originates from China. This shows the risks faced by the global economy towards maintaining a resilient global supply chain against calls for fragmentation and increased protectionism. There is a need to heighten the focus towards working intensely on global trade agreements that will facilitate a more connected and diversified globalized supply chain. As we are now seated in a phase of slowed growth, any supply chain vulnerability can disproportionately affect the prospects primarily of the emerging and less-developed economies, and dampen the decades of impressive progress in moving towards the realization of the Sustainable Development Goals (SDGs) agreed to in the UN.

Meanwhile, the rise of new technologies offers a fertile arena with numerous possibilities for economic progress. As we gradually leave the industrial era which dominated the last two centuries, a digital era is firmly standing at our doorstep and is poised to shape our future in ways we cannot yet fully see. The internet has already embedded itself as a crucial part of the daily lives of significant populations across the world, and we are quickly moving into years where artificial intelligence will be ubiquitous, quantum computing will bring new revolutionary possibilities, and synthetic biology might start changing fundamental aspects of our lives.

THE NEED FOR CALCULATED REFORMS

Achieving domination in these technologies is now on the agenda of all major economies. So far, the United States is the pre-eminent innovation power, but it is increasingly being challenged not only by China but also by global networks of innovation where the power of rising countries like India is bound to grow. The countries that educate their human talent, commit themselves to research and development, and develop an open entrepreneurial culture will be the ones to avail the greatest possibilities in the decades that are before us.

Leapfrogging towards dominance in new technologies also demands coordinated policy formulation to match the momentum of expanding innovation. There are bound to be issues which we cannot foresee as of today, making policy cohesion an imperative for a smooth transition towards an era of rapid technological advancement. As the AI revolution starts to accelerate, questions on the possibility of finding agreement on a common global framework or structure for setting the standards, principles and limitations around AI have started featuring on international forums. There is very little disagreement on the need for this to happen but far less agreement on how and by whom this can be done.

A similar institutional incapacity to facilitate swift policy responses was evident in our global health architecture when we failed to secure more equitable access to the life-saving vaccines in the initial stages of the COVID-19 pandemic that took the lives of tens of millions of people around the world. We were lucky to find vaccines with a speed not seen before, owing to the scientific advancements facilitating a rapid development of the necessary production capacity, but our policy responses to equity in vaccine-sharing were not as efficient as our scientific feat. The COVID pandemic is unlikely to be the last, and the next one could well be as contagious and significantly more deadly. Intense international work is underway to update the rules and structures of global health cooperation and deliberate on contentious issues like vaccine equity, but whether this will be sufficient to meet the next pandemic is very much an open question.

To these must of course be added the challenge of climate change. What is needed to meet the goals set in the Paris Agreement of limiting the temperature rise to 1.5 degrees is nothing less than moving away from the fossil fuels that drove the centuries of industrial development, and to do so within just a couple of decades. The challenge before emerging economies is enormous, and that before humanity is even bigger. The older powers of the US and Europe are responsible for most of the emissions already accumulated in the atmosphere, but the rising economies of China and India carry the heaviest responsibility for the emissions now and in the decades ahead. A massive change is required in the structure of the global economy and fuel consumption patterns of billions of people. Tensions will be there. A siloed economic approach focusing on protectionism poses friction towards an accelerated and cost-effective green transition. The resistance to ironing out differences among manufacturing economies of green technologies like EVs and photovoltaic cells and those economies that are aggressively looking to transition to greener energy is one of the challenges which will shape the trajectory of global policy responses. Whether coordinated efforts on transitioning away from non-renewables which have produced the Dubai Consensus achieved at the COP28 will elicit sufficient global cooperation on these issues is difficult to guess at the time of writing.

All of these are issues that have figured prominently on the agenda of the Raisina Dialogue over the years, and the discussions have been characterized by the fact that they have curated varied perspectives from across the world. It has not been just an Indian dialogue but truly a global one, where the younger voices from around the world are also given a prominent role. In a world challenged by geopolitical, geoeconomic and geotechnological fissures, the Raisina Dialogue 2024 has all the potential to be even more interesting as we face an evermore challenging world where the need for global cooperation becomes paramount.

Section 2

Shared Visions:
Unbreakable Bilateral Ties

Penny Wong

Minister for Foreign Affairs of Australia

Bonds Down Under: The Dynamic Tapestry of the Australia–India Relationship

WHEN THE RAISINA DIALOGUE WAS CONCEIVED, THE world was already experiencing heightened disruption and the global order was already under considerable strain. As we enter the tenth year since the annual Dialogue was imagined, the context for these meetings has become ever more serious. We see more and more conflict in the world. Tensions in the Indo–Pacific have risen between states with overlapping claims and disputed borders. Compounding the challenges are dangerous encounters on land, in the air, and at sea.

We all know that the region we live in is being reshaped. The only question is whether we choose to play our part in the reshaping, or let others decide our future.

Against this background, the need for forums like the Raisina Dialogue has never been greater and the wisdom behind its inception has never been clearer. The Raisina Dialogue has rightly become one of the Indo–Pacific's premier gatherings on geopolitics and geoeconomics, drawing leaders in government, business, media and civil society.

It is no coincidence that the conference was founded and is being held in India—a country that is central to regional stability. Like India, the Raisina Dialogue has become a centre of gravity for strategic thinking in the region. The

Observer Research Foundation has also expanded its reach to other countries, including Australia: Australia hosted the first Raisina@Sydney in 2023, and External Affairs Minister S. Jaishankar and I announced in late 2023 that Australia would host Raisina Down Under in 2024.

To mark this important milestone for the Raisina Dialogue, I am pleased to share my reflections on how we avert war and maintain peace—and more than that, how Australia and India are working to preserve a region that reflects our national interests and our shared regional interests. Our close collaboration in this endeavour is only made possible by the great strides that Australia and India have taken in our bilateral relationship in recent years.

A REGIONAL BALANCE OF POWER

Australia looks to shape a region that is peaceful, stable and prosperous. Our interests lie in a region that operates by rules, standards and norms—where a larger country does not determine the fate of a smaller one; where each country can pursue its own aspirations, its own prosperity.

Australia is working in a range of forums to enable this stability. It was at Raisina in 2020 that a trilateral research project made the case for deeper cooperation between India, Australia and Indonesia. Since becoming the foreign minister, I have had the privilege of attending regular trilateral meetings with my counterparts from Indonesia and India.

Australia, working with India and partners, is contributing to the balance of power that keeps the peace in the region. We know that strategic competition is operating on several levels. Domains that may have historically been considered separate—economic, diplomatic, strategic, military—are all interwoven, and all framed by an intense contest of narratives.

The challenges we face are not just the potential of

kinetic conflict on our shores. Coercive trade measures; unsustainable lending; political interference; disinformation; and reshaping international rules, standards and norms that have benefited smaller countries, from trade to human rights—these all encroach on the ability of countries to exercise their agency, contribute to regional balance, and decide their own destiny. They constrain sovereignty. And while sovereignty might be exercised alone, it is best assured when we are working together. Because none of us can achieve a region we seek by ourselves.

The less unified we are and the less we all operate by the same rules, the more likely it is that vulnerabilities will be exploited. This is why Australia is committed to strong partnerships like the Quad and to mutually agreed rules that enable more stability and choices, which in turn translate to greater autonomy and sovereignty.

Just as each country has a responsibility to help maintain conditions for peace, we also have a responsibility to play our part in the collective deterrence of aggression. By having strong defence capabilities of our own, and by working with partners investing in their own capabilities, we change the calculus for any potential aggressor. Our foreign and defence policies are two essential and interdependent parts of Australia's approach to statecraft. Both of these fundamental pillars are debated and discussed in New Delhi during the Raisina Dialogue.

PARTNERING WITH INDIA

For Australia, working with India to shape the region that we want is a key priority. India's prosperity matters to Australia, just as Australia's prosperity matters to India. This is not only because of the immense strategic weight and importance of India in the region and the world. Geography may have decided that we share regional interests, but we have decided to be friends. This was a choice, one that speaks to our shared future and reflects our shared history.

Fifty years ago, in 1973, Australia's Labor Prime Minister Gough Whitlam visited India. It was the first visit to India by an Australian Prime Minister in 14 years. Whitlam said at the time, 'Here are two great democracies bordering the Indian Ocean, both members of the Commonwealth, both deeply dedicated to world peace, both with federal systems, both holding great institutions in common.'[1]

Yet, understanding the need for deep ties between our countries goes back even further than Prime Minister Whitlam's visit. In 1949, India's Prime Minister Jawaharlal Nehru and Australia's Prime Minister Ben Chifley met in London, at the Commonwealth Prime Ministers' Conference. At the time, Prime Minister Nehru wanted India to both become a republic and maintain its membership within the Commonwealth. Prime Minister Chifley was one of the few supporters of his cause. Nehru and Chifley would speak of each other with great admiration in the years that followed. We take forward this tradition with the Albanese government, recognizing the importance of India to the region and the world. Our prime ministers met five times last year, including once in Sydney and twice in India.

India and Australia are working together through our Comprehensive Strategic Partnership, through the Quad, and through regional architecture and the multilateral system. We are growing our economic partnership and looking to deepen two-way trade and investment, including by negotiating an ambitious Comprehensive Economic Cooperation Agreement. We are also launching new climate

---

[1]Lee, David. *Mediating Middle Powers: Shaw, Grant, Curtis and Upton, 1972–83.* ANU Press. https://tinyurl.com/2rjvxp8d. Accessed on 14 August 2024.

initiatives in green steel and hydrogen, critical minerals and innovation and technology. The close cooperation between Australia and India that Prime Minister Whitlam envisaged has come to pass.

The relationship also benefits from the legacy of Prime Minister Whitlam's changes to the immigration policy of Australia. Half of the Australian population was born overseas or has a parent who was born overseas; that includes me. It means that when Australians look across the world, we see ourselves, just as the world sees itself reflected in us. One in every 25 Australians claims Indian heritage—our fastest-growing and second-largest diaspora community.

We celebrate this history and this heritage. We launched the Centre for Australia–India Relations during Prime Minister Modi's visit to Australia in May, at an event attended by some 20,000 members of the diaspora. The Centre is harnessing the energy and knowledge of Australia's Indian community to improve our economic and political links. The 850,000 Indian tourists and students that visit Australia each year also contribute to this goal.

Australia also launched the new Maitri Fellowships program, which will enable Indian researchers to spend six months to two years at an Australian think tank, and Australian researchers to spend six months in India. We recognize the important role that think tanks, civil society and other stakeholders play in this relationship, as well as the power and influence of conferences such as the Raisina Dialogue that provide a platform for debate. The Raisina Young Fellows Programme, supported by the Australian government, is another way in which this forum is developing and providing opportunities to emerging scholars and mid-career officials alike.

Australia and India have a proud history as democracies that foster academic excellence and a broad range of views. At a time when pluralism and democracy are being challenged worldwide, the next generation of Indians and Australians have a particular responsibility to strengthen the institutions that we hold dear.

We believe that our multicultural democracy and the pluralism that accompanies it are essential to our ability to shape the region we live in. I have the privilege of serving alongside the most diverse parliament in Australia's history. We believe this diversity is one of our greatest strengths.

The challenges that we face today in our region and in the world have prompted comparisons with 1914, the 1930s and 1962. Those comparisons should serve as warnings, but nothing more. We are not hostages to history. We decide what to do with the present. We are active players in our region, not just to guard against the consequences of regional contests, but to shape and influence it to advance our national and shared interests.

The Raisina Dialogue has always focused on the gravest challenges of our time. Today military power is expanding, but measures to avoid military conflict are not—and there are insufficient concrete mechanisms for averting it. The risk of conflict is of deep concern to us all.

That is why Australia continues to encourage mutual strategic reassurance, military risk-reduction measures, and open lines of communication at all levels. Anyone with the privilege of a platform such as the office that I hold, or a conference like Raisina, should feel compelled to press for the responsible management of global-power competition. This is in the interest of all of us with an existential stake in regional peace and stability.

The global community comes together at the Raisina Dialogue to debate these issues. It is a key opportunity for the world's leaders and thinkers to develop ideas for progress and prosperity. The success of this forum in

New Delhi shows the seriousness with which India takes its role in the Indo–Pacific region. It also reflects the unprecedented circumstances that we face. As we chart a way forward, the need for the Raisina Dialogue, and the ideas that flow from it, will only grow.

Prince Faisal bin Farhan Al Saud

Minister of Foreign Affairs in Saudi Arabia

India and Saudi Arabia: A Thriving Partnership towards a Promising Future

RELATIONS BETWEEN INDIA AND THE ARAB WORLD DATE back centuries. Historic interactions between the Arab and Islamic world and India resulted in lasting cultural linkages between us. Flourishing through trade—from the time Arab merchants ventured into Indian spice trade—and rooted in human connections, sustained engagement between our nations has brought us closer. Enhanced trade gave way to increased cultural exchange and knowledge transfer. Global challenges and a synergy of interests intersected to produce a robust strategic partnership between India and the Kingdom of Saudi Arabia. We, in the Kingdom, believe this partnership will only grow stronger, through deeper and broader engagement.

At the core of any thriving relationship is its human element. The friendship between both countries sustains our cooperation and enables more cultural exchange. More people from India visited the Kingdom in the past year than ever before. In 2022, nearly one million travellers from India travelled to the Kingdom. By the end of 2023, this figure increased by 52.68 per cent, nearing 1.7 million visitors; we are targeting 12 million visitors by 2030. The average number of inbound flights in 2023 reached 256 per week (a 25 per cent increase from 2022), and we are aiming to increase inbound flights from India to 290 per week. Indian nationals residing in the Kingdom form its largest expatriate group, contributing value and further strengthening the friendship between our nations through cultural engagement.

Realizing the strategic importance of this relationship, the leadership in both countries is determined to take this decades-long partnership to new heights of collaboration, unlocking the immense potential it holds, not only for our two nations but also for the health and resilience of the global economy. In today's interconnected world where challenges and threats transcend borders, it is incumbent upon us, as leading regional and international actors, and integral G20 members, to leverage our partnership and international position to enhance shared efforts towards a future that prioritizes cooperation over confrontation and development over conflict. We are highly motivated to work towards a prosperous future which meets the expectations of our populations, especially the youth in both countries.

Both our countries carry significant weight within the global economic architecture. As leading G20 members, this weight underpins the importance of developing trade and investment relations, and the value this can generate on the world stage, jointly addressing issues varying from food and energy security to supply chain resilience and facilitating investments.

We were pleased to take part in the successful G20 summit held in New Delhi in September 2023, which witnessed the announcement of an MOU to establish the India–Middle East–Europe Corridor (IMEC)—an ambitious cross-continental project which will link West Asia and the Middle East to Europe via rail and shipping lines. The IMEC will comprise two separate corridors: the East corridor, connecting India to the Arabian Gulf, and the Northern corridor from the Middle East to Europe.

This massive project will significantly impact growth and development in the global economy, owing to the planned upgrade in infrastructure, connectivity, flow of goods, and economic integration. In addition, the MOU includes building pipelines that comprise high-efficiency, reliable cross-border data transmission cables, as well as enhancing energy security, through a development of green transit corridors to export electricity and hydrogen.

From a bilateral perspective, trade relations have been on an upward trajectory in recent years. In 2022, bilateral trade reached $52 billion, registering a 23 per cent increase over the previous year. Figures are still holding strong for 2023, indicating that bilateral trade by the end of the year's third quarter is estimated to have exceeded $35 billion. Also, in 2022, both India and the Kingdom achieved the highest growth rates among G20 countries. Both countries maintained positive growth levels during that year, with India recording 6.3 per cent GDP growth, exceeding G7 economies for two successive years. The positive indicators and sustained growth projections in both countries underscore the integral positions they occupy within the global economy.

The visit of Mohamad Bin Salman Al Saud, Crown Prince and Prime Minister of the Kingdom of Saudi Arabia, to India in September 2023 sought to solidify and deepen the bonds of friendship and strategic partnership between our two nations. It was an opportunity to review and reflect on the developments in cooperation since the PM's previous visit in February 2019, as well as PM Narendra Modi's historic visit to the Kingdom in October of the same year. These visits resulted in the formation of the Strategic Partnership Council (SPC) as the highest cooperation mechanism governing bilateral relations and aimed to open up new avenues of cooperation in diverse sectors. Prime Minister Modi's visit signified a leap in the strategic partnership in both bilateral and multilateral cooperation.

The first meeting of the SPC was convened in September, during which we reviewed the tremendous progress achieved in the ministerial committees, sub-committees and working groups. The council is concerned with deepening cooperation in fields of mutual interest. My visit to New Delhi for the Raisina Dialogue in February 2024 also presented an opportunity to oversee additional agreements and MOUs in many fields, including energy, bilateral investment, digitization and electronic manufacturing, among others.

HARNESSING THE LIMITLESS POTENTIAL

We have worked together to facilitate more trade and investment between both countries. The effectiveness of such cooperation contributed to India becoming the Kingdom's second largest trading partner, and the Kingdom securing its position as India's fourth largest trading partner by 2023. Total investments by the Saudi Public Investment Fund in India reached $3.3 billion.

There is potential for further growth, as both nations offer valuable products across several sectors. Current areas of cooperation focus on energy, renewable energy, transfer of energy, hydrogen production, petrochemicals and fertilizers, carbon capture and reuse technologies, technologies associated with the circular carbon economy, food security, technology, services and logistics. The focus on energy sectors stem from the Kingdom's leading role as a reliable and responsible energy producer.

In addition, the Kingdom has been implementing widespread policy reform to enable the success of its national development plans. This promises to encourage widespread opportunities for collaboration in all sectors and within diverse segments (whether between governments, businesses, or even small and medium enterprises). The way in which India has been developing its tech industry is also an important area of collaboration. In short, avenues of cooperation are numerous and the potential is limitless.

Continuing to develop and nurture our bilateral relationship can translate into further engagement for India in the Arab Gulf region and the wider Arab world, where there is ample appetite for partnerships that advance inter-regional connectivity and mutual development. Indeed, India is an integral partner across the Gulf, capitalizing on bilateral and multilateral partnerships. The Joint Economics and Investments Committee, comprising Ministers of Commerce, is a key example of how institutional frameworks can help advance cooperation between India and the region.

However, for development efforts to reach sustainable results, we must maintain secure and stable conditions whereby regional security complements the push towards development and attracting investments. In line with Vision 2030, the Kingdom's foreign policy has focused on leveraging its partnerships to enhance regional security and stability, which will, in turn, encourage longevity in strategic partnerships. As a trusted partner, India's constructive engagement is valued by the Kingdom and across the region. We are eagerly developing both political and economic aspects of our cooperation. From our end, the Saudi–Indian partnership remains robust and forward-looking. We are eyeing, through our ever-developing relations, a bright and prosperous future for both nations.

In conclusion, I would also like to acknowledge ORF's efforts, which are known to generate valuable research and dialogue around key policy issues. The Raisina Dialogue is an important platform that enables engagement with officials and leaders in corporate and non-governmental sectors. It discusses challenges and issues of international concern, with a view to resolving them. I am confident that this publication, through a variety of perspectives within its articles, will reflect the rich discussions that occurred.

Tadashi Maeda

*Chairman, Japan Bank for
International Cooperation*

The Japan–India Vision: Looking back, Looking ahead

MY FIRST CONTACT WITH THE OBSERVER RESEARCH Foundation (ORF) was when I presented a conference jointly organized by ORF and International Institute for Strategic Studies (IISS) in New Delhi. Thereafter, in 2020, the Japan Bank for International Cooperation (JBIC) began an engagement with ORF to strengthen its intelligence capabilities around South Asia. I was then invited to the Raisina Dialogue for the first time in 2021, held virtually during the COVID-19 pandemic, where I joined a panel with Tony Abbott, the former Australian Prime Minister. More importantly, I have a long relationship with India's External Affairs Minister S. Jaishankar, whose strong initiatives for the conference were a big reason for me to participate at the Raisina Dialogue.

My first in-person attendance at Raisina was in 2022, when I attended a panel discussion about investments in quality infrastructure. I also attended a Raisina fireside chat and was interviewed about Japanese economic statecraft. I was then invited to become an ORF Global Advisory Board Member, an offer I accepted without any hesitation.

I had also worked with IISS as a council member for global strategic events, including the Shangri-La

Dialogue and the Manama Dialogue. While the Shangri-La Dialogue mainly focuses on defence security issues, the Raisina Dialogue covers a broader range of global topics, including advanced technology, environmental and social considerations, economic security and economic statecraft. The unique, holistic agenda and the diverse and distinguished participants at the Raisina Dialogue are exceptional and impressive.

In 2023, I again visited Delhi for the 8th Raisina Dialogue. Having enjoyed a panel discussion with Prime Minister Abbott and Rajeev Chandrasekhar, India's minister of state for electronics and information technology, I discussed with the ORF leadership an ambitious plan to hold Raisina@Tokyo in the near future.

Raisina@Tokyo Japan is now being planned by JBIC, ORF and Keizai Doyukai (Japan Association of Corporate Executives), with leaders from India, Japan and other like-minded countries invited to discuss strategic issues. I believe such a new initiative led by India and Japan will foster more strategic relationships and achieve new heights for relations between the two countries through its unique perspective and rich inspiration from Japan, which held the G7 presidency in 2023.

INDIA'S ROLE

Now that the world is in the midst of a chaotic situation, India's role in the global order is even more critical. Through the Raisina Dialogue, the global community can attain rich knowledge and information about 'India Inc.', specifically its strategic intentions and willingness as a responsible regional and global power and a leader of the Global South.

Economic security has been a priority for Japanese Prime Minister Fumio Kishida, as reflected by the creation of a new cabinet position dedicated to economic security in 2022, with Takayuki Kobayashi serving as its minister. The Kishida government then set up a promotion council to draft legislation outlining economic security goals. Finally, it appointed a private sector advisory group to help refine those goals and to prioritize government planning. Keizai Doyukai also weighed in, urging the government to remain in close contact with private actors that it could oversee as it sought to enhance economic security. I was appointed as the chairperson of the Global South India Committee, newly established in Keizai Doyukai, and I am keen to play a leading role in fostering understanding among key Japanese players about the recent business environment and opportunities and issues in India.

While the world is yet to recover from the COVID-19 pandemic, and global real GDP is forecast to grow by only 2.2 per cent in 2023, India has overtaken the UK to become the world's fifth-largest economy. It achieved a strong recovery, with 7.2 per cent growth in 2022–23, and is now targeting continuous 6 per cent growth in FY 2023–24. India's emerging consumer market and its huge industrial potential for global supply chains have made it an increasingly important investment destination for multinationals in diverse sectors, such as information technology, electronics, pharmaceuticals and renewables.

As Japan took up the mantle of leadership of the G7, and being the only Asian member of the G7, Japan's presidency had worked more intently with a rising India, which had the presidency of G20. It was in Japan's interests to utilize its G7 presidency to strengthen its relationship with India and synergize a cooperative framework. India also held a virtual summit with the leaders of African and Asian countries, aptly called the Voice of the Global South, to hear out their problems and later present these at the G20 Summit.

Eventually, as India and Japan have successfully presided over the G7 and G20, they will collaborate in future to synergize their efforts to combat pressing global challenges.

India and Japan share strong economic ties, and trade between the two was worth US$20.57 billion in FY 2021–22. Our two countries have surpassed their previous target of 3.5 trillion yen in Japanese investment during 2014–19, and have set an investment target of US$42 billion from Japan to India in the next five years, which was announced after the fourteenth annual summit held in 2022.

India and Japan share a similar outlook on regional security, economic growth and strategic interests. In recent years, the relationship has evolved into a strategic partnership, with both nations collaborating on various fronts including defence, security, trade, investments and technology. In the current geopolitical scenario, the Indo–Pacific region has emerged as a focal point of global attention, and India and Japan are at the forefront of efforts to maintain stability in the region.

Japan's Free and Open Indo–Pacific strategy and India's Indo–Pacific Oceans Initiative have provided the framework for the two countries to deepen their strategic partnership and cooperation in the region. With the upscaling of the Quad between the US, Australia and our two countries, India and Japan's growing ties in the Indo–Pacific are grounded in a shared commitment to multilateralism and strengthening the rules-based order.

Another critical aspect in the 'Japan and India Vision 2025',[1] which seeks synergy between India's 'Act East' policy and Japan's 'Partnership for Quality Infrastructure', is the

---

[1]'Japan and India Vision 2025 Special Strategic and Global Partnership', *Ministry of Foreign Affairs of Japan*, 12 December 2015, https://tinyurl.com/bdhtu4ch. Accessed on 12 August 2024.

intention expressed by the two nations to promote quality infrastructure to augment connectivity in the region.

In March 2023, Japan first unveiled its vision for a 'Bay of Bengal–Northeast India industrial value chain concept' during a key policy speech delivered by Prime Minister Kishida in New Delhi. Under this concept, Japan will view Bangladesh and other areas of the South as an integrated single economic zone and will promote the 'Bay of Bengal–Northeast India industrial value chain concept' in cooperation with India and Bangladesh. To foster growth in the entire region, Japan will encourage business leaders to take a 'fresh look at India's Northeast, to fully harness its potential'.[2] Japan is looking ahead to collaborate closely with India and contribute to stability in the South Asian region.

JBIC'S ACTIONS IN INDIA

Since 2020, JBIC has mobilized US$13 billion for India together with our co-financial partners. Addressing the dynamic global environment, JBIC has been leveraging the strengths of Japanese companies and aligning its operations based on the global priorities of host countries. India has undertaken several reforms to revitalize investment in the manufacturing sector, such as ease of doing business, demystifying labour and tax laws, and strengthening insolvency and bankruptcy laws. Bolstered by these reforms, Japan's Nippon Steel Corporation, in partnership with ArcelorMittal S.A. of Luxembourg, acquired distressed Essar Steel Limited at an insolvency and bankruptcy proceeding. To support this merger and acquisition and the Make in

---

[2]Laskar, Rezul H., 'Japan to help build industrial value chain linking B'desh port, India's Northeast', *Hindustan Times*, 19 May 2023, https://tinyurl.com/yxhn34bj. Accessed on 12 August 2024.

India initiative, in March 2020, JBIC mobilized a financing of US$5,000 million to revitalize and expand the renamed ArcelorMittal Nippon Steel India Limited. Subsequently, in March 2023, JBIC further mobilized another US$5,000 million to finance investment in capacity expansion of an integrated steel facility from 9 mtpa to 15 mtpa in Hazira, Gujarat, to meet the growing steel demand in India.

Amid the raging COVID-19 pandemic, the first Quad Leadership Summit was held in March 2021, where leaders of Japan, Australia, India and the US identified the response to the pandemic as the most urgent global challenge. In this context, being a policy lending financial institution, JBIC committed US$100 million to the Export Import Bank of India to enhance investments in the healthcare sector related to COVID-19, including vaccines and treatment drugs.

The COVID-19 pandemic cracked wide open fractured global supply chains, which forced the industrial sector to review and optimize the global supply chain that was facing growing geopolitical risks and uncertainties. In 2020, when economic activities were stagnating due to pandemic restrictions, the Indian government proactively announced several economic measures to sustain liquidity and stimulate manufacturing. To supplement these measures and strengthen the resilience of the supply chains of Japanese automobile manufacturers in India, JBIC extended a total of US$2,000 million to the State Bank of India in October 2020 and March 2021 to promote the smooth flow of funds for the manufacturing and sales businesses of suppliers and dealers of Japanese automobile manufacturers, as well as for the provision of auto loans for the purchase of Japanese automobiles.

Consequently, a similar support of US$100 million was established with IndusInd Bank in March 2023 to enhance the supply chain resilience of Japanese construction equipment manufacturers in India, which was necessary for expanding the development of India's infrastructure and the strengthening of local small- and medium-sized suppliers, dealers, contractors and others.

JBIC is also at the forefront of leading Japanese companies' initiatives to address global challenges, especially concerning the transition towards a decarbonized society. In India, JBIC has been supporting energy transition initiatives of public and private sector companies using advanced Japanese technologies. In October 2020, JBIC extended a loan of JPY 50 billion to NTPC Limited to diversify its generation mix by adding solar power generation projects and addressing elevated air pollution by supporting the installation of environmental equipment projects. JBIC also partnered with Power Finance Corporation by setting up a JPY 30 billion line of credit to support renewable energy projects and energy-efficient power generation projects in India. Additional support of JPY 15 billion was extended to SJVN Limited in March 2023 for its solar power generation projects in India.

Finally, JBIC promotes equity investment as a multifunctional development financial institution. India and Japan have been undertaking multiple initiatives, including the India–Japan Clean Energy Partnership, to promote environmental preservation efforts in India, and in August 2023, JBIC and India's National Infrastructure Investment Fund established a bilateral India–Japan Fund under the India–Japan Clean and Growth Platform. The fund will enable the injection of equity investment in ambitious and promising projects with a Japan nexus in clean and growth-oriented sectors all over India.

Admiral Sir Tony Radakin

Chief of the Defence Staff of the United Kingdom

Strengthening the UK–India Relationship: Navigating Global Challenges through Collaboration and Partnership

THE 2020s FEEL LIKE A NEW AND EXCITING CHAPTER IN the vital relationship between Britain and India. When Rishi Sunak became our first Hindu prime minister in October 2022, one of his first telephone calls was to Prime Minister Narendra Modi, in which the two men reflected on the 'living bridge' between our countries. It is a bridge that brings us together in all sorts of ways, most obviously through family links—1.8 million people of Indian heritage live in Britain—but also through business, trade, education, science, arts, culture and sports, and increasingly through defence and security too.

These relationships reflect the diplomatic and commercial ties that are the legacy of our long and complex colonial history. But increasingly, they also reflect a more contemporary dynamic based on a relationship of equals and a shared adherence to a set of universal values and common interests that guide our approach to global affairs.

That does not mean India and the United Kingdom (UK) are always aligned. Our interests and perspectives are naturally different; but the fact that we acknowledge and respect these differences is a sign of the maturity of our relationship. As an example, I was struck by the recent comment by India's Minister of External Affairs S. Jaishankar when he said that 'Europe needs to grow out of the mindset that our problems are the world's problems, but the world's problems are not Europe's problems.'[1] There is a good deal of truth in that, particularly when we consider the impact of climate change on countries bordering the Indian Ocean, or our struggle to roll out COVID vaccines to the whole world. Britain and the West should listen to India out of respect and because there is much for us to learn by doing so.

This explains, in part, why India and the UK have taken different approaches to Russia's war in Ukraine. India and other non-aligned countries inevitably view events in Europe through a different historical and geopolitical lens. The Commonwealth Memorial Gates in London—which commemorate the five million volunteers from the Indian subcontinent, Africa and the Caribbean who fought in World Wars I and II—is a poignant reminder of why former colonial nations may be wary of entanglement in the affairs of Europe.

Yet I would argue the conflict in Ukraine is more than 'just another' European border dispute. Indeed, for Ukraine, this is an anti-colonial struggle that should matter to the whole world. Russian President Vladimir Putin considers Ukraine a wayward territory of historic Greater Russia, and the notions of sovereign borders, self-determination and democratic mandates matter little to him. He does not care that the former Soviet states have a sovereign right to determine their own future, and to choose their own allies. He simply believed he could take what he wanted, and

---

[1] 'EAM S Jaishankar on why Europe's perspective of world's problem is flawed', *YouTube*, 3 June 2022. https://tinyurl.com/4fb625hm. Accessed on 14 August 2024.

nobody would stop him; the subsequent war crimes, sham referendums, arbitrary detentions and forced relocations speak to a wider contempt for human rights and civilized values, as does the nuclear rhetoric. This sense of impunity has been the pattern of Putin's behaviour for the past 20 years: from the downing of a Malaysian airlines jet to radiological poisonings on British soil; from mercenaries in Mali to the reckless use of cluster munitions and incendiary weapons in Syria.

This struggle is already global, rather than regional, in character. It was notable that in the same week that Chinese President Xi Jinping visited Moscow to cement China's 'no-limits partnership' with Russia, Japanese Prime Minister Fumio Kishida made a surprise visit to Kyiv. Certainly the consequences of Russia's aggression have been felt worldwide, and it is the world's poorest that have suffered most, whether through the shortages that flow from disruption to global food and energy supplies, or the inflation that is being experienced around the world. This explains the extraordinary international response over the past year, with 143 countries voting to condemn Russia's invasion at the UN, 40 offering military and economic aid to Ukraine, and 30 imposing sanctions on Russia. These countries recognize that Russia's aggression is more than a brutal assault on a neighbouring country; it is an attack on the rules and standards of behaviour that underpin security and stability worldwide.

President Putin is not alone in seeking to challenge the global order. Last year, the Royal Navy intercepted shipments of advanced weaponry smuggled out of Iran. They included components for the kind of land attack missiles that have been used by Houthi forces to strike targets in Saudi Arabia and the United Arab Emirates. Meanwhile, North Korea conducted more than 90 missile tests, and the Kim regime has threatened to turn the Pacific into 'a shooting range'. Iran and North Korea are both supporting Russian aggression in Ukraine, the latter supplying long-range attack drones. We have also seen a far more aggressive stance from China in the South China Sea and the Taiwan Strait, including military drills simulating a blockade of Taiwan. The UK does not see China as an acute threat like Russia, but we are clear-eyed about what Prime Minister Sunak terms a 'systemic challenge' to our values and interests and our economic security.

This degree of challenge and volatility in the world poses a set of questions for democratic countries like Britain and India. If the autocracies of the world think they can act with impunity, are responsible nations like ours ready to respond, and if so, how?

INTEGRATED REVIEW

The UK's answer to this question is found in our *Integrated Review of Security, Defence, Development and Foreign Policy*, first published in 2021 and updated in March 2023 to reflect a world that has shifted from being competitive to becoming actively contested. The main conclusion of the review is that responsible nations must work even harder to out-cooperate and out-compete those states that are driving instability.

For the UK, this effort begins in the Euro–Atlantic . The review reaffirmed the threat posed by Russia and singled out NATO as the UK's most important foreign policy commitment, but the review is also clear that our interests do not stop at the Suez Canal. The UK is a nuclear power, with a permanent seat in the UN Security Council. It is a member of the G7, a leader in science, technology and higher education, and a cultural superpower. For all these reasons, the UK's outlook is global rather than regional.

Economic opportunity explains our decision to seek ASEAN dialogue partner status and why we recently became the first European country to join the Trans-Pacific Partnership. But we recognize that security and prosperity are intertwined, and with economic opportunity comes the expectation—and the responsibility—to contribute to the freedoms and security that underpin the region's stability. This is why, for example, we actively exercise the right of innocent passage in the South China Sea and the Taiwan Strait, since the freedom of navigation matters to global prosperity here every bit as much as it does in the Black Sea or the English Channel.

The 2021 passage of the UK Carrier Strike Group to the Indo–Pacific indicated our desire for more regular deployments to the region (Prime Minister Sunak recently announced that it would be returning in 2025). It also opened the way for Konkan Shakti, the first tri-service exercise between the UK and India. The UK will also increasingly base more capabilities in the region, building on our existing footprint in Oman, Nepal, Brunei and Diego Garcia, and the facilities available to us in Singapore to provide a more enduring and consistent presence. Later this year, we will establish a Littoral Response Group in the Indian Ocean, consisting of Royal Marines, Commando Helicopters and Amphibious Shipping. I expect this to create new opportunities to train with India, at sea and ashore. By 2030, the British Armed Forces will have the broadest, most integrated presence in the region of any European power.

But our presence is far larger than our naval and military footprint. It reflects a maximalist approach to our national security that aligns the work of the British Armed Forces even more closely with our trading ambitions and with our domestic strengths in science and security. This is exemplified by our Global Combat Air Programme to develop a sixth-generation fighter with Italy and Japan, and by the AUKUS agreement with the US and Australia. In entering such partnerships, we bind ourselves together industrially, technologically and militarily, and also in the way we respond to the security challenges of our time.

THE UK–INDIA PARTNERSHIP

But what of the defence partnership between Britain and India? What is the extent of our ambition? And what are the 'big ideas' in defence and security that can bring us closer together over the coming decades?

As two of the world's leading economic powers, reliant on seaborne trade, we have steadily increased cooperation on maritime security in recent years. This includes an agreement to share information on grey and dark shipping and active participation in Prime Minister Modi's Indo–Pacific Oceans Initiative. But we are ready to do more. The UK has a depth and breadth of expertise to contribute—in hydrography and international maritime law, from our experience of counterpiracy operations in East Africa, and our role in information sharing and multi-agency integration in UK waters.

There is growing cooperation in air and land as well as maritime. In March, Exercise Cobra Warrior saw five Mirage aircraft and two C-17s from the Indian Air Force visit the UK for four weeks to train alongside the Royal Air Force and other partner nations. The following month, Indian Army personnel arrived in the UK for Exercise Ajeya Warrior with the British Army, now in its seventh iteration.

It is natural that our industry-to-industry collaboration is also growing, with avenues of cooperation including integrated electric propulsion for ships and advanced core technology for jet engines. As India seeks to strengthen its own sovereign defence industry, there is a huge amount that the UK's defence sector can contribute, for example in the underwater battlespace and with air and missile defence, lightweight tanks, modern fighter aircraft and helicopters.

Finally, there is the challenge of reform and modernization. The Ukraine crisis has underlined the importance of speed and agility required to introduce new equipment into service, the resilience of our stockpiles, and our ability to mobilize the entire defence enterprise, including industry, around our objectives, and to do so at pace. The UK's Integrated Review was backed by increased investment in the armed forces, which allows us to address these issues and become more lethal, more agile, smarter, and more sophisticated across the traditional domains, or land, sea, and air, and the new domains of cyber and space.

Not all these challenges are the same for India. Our armed forces are structured differently, but we have more in common than we think. After all, our countries are two of only six with the expertise, capacity and ambition to build and operate nuclear submarines and aircraft carriers, the hallmarks of global military powers, and together, India and the UK face the same simple dilemma—as modern warfare becomes ever faster, as the threats multiply and become more complex, how do we stay ahead of our competitors?

I would suggest the answer lies in the power and relevance of military and industrial partnership, and the need to strengthen and defend the international rules-based system wherever it is being challenged—a task that India and the UK are ideally placed to support.

Scott Morrison

Former Prime Minister of Australia

Through 'Maitri' and 'Mateship'

THE HINDI WORD *MAITRI* MEANS THE ABILITY TO WORK side by side and trust each other. In Australia, we use the word 'mateship' when referring to our special relationships. Whichever word we choose, Australia and India have been friends for a long time, and for good reason. This friendship has become even closer and more substantive and strategically significant in recent times.

An important part of any friendship is seeing the world through your partner's eyes. While Australia and India have much in common, such as our commitment to representative parliamentary democracy and the rule of law, there are also many differences. Our geography, politics, cultural and religious history, economic challenges and opportunities, each tell different stories. Good partners work hard to understand and respect their differences as much as their similarities. In Australia and India's case, these differences are not obstacles or a cause for tension in our relationship, even where there is disagreement. Rather, our differences represent an opportunity to combine discrete strengths and perspectives to successfully address our shared goals.

To this end, the Raisina Dialogue has always been an important opportunity for Australia, and many Western partners, to stop and look at the world through an Indian lens and test our own Western strategic outlook against this viewpoint. India's role as a leader of the new Global South reinforces the importance of such an exercise to gain insights on how to improve the effectiveness of the engagement of Western democracies with the Global South, particularly India. Fundamental to this understanding is appreciating the priority, rightly placed, by developing countries in the Global South on economic development to strengthen their own sovereignty.

REMINISCENCES OF A PRODUCTIVE PAST

As Prime Minister, I always placed a high priority on supporting India's economic goals in addressing our partnership. I still do. India's economic success is critical to our own future prosperity and the broader strategic balance of the Indo–Pacific region. Such growth, as Prime Minister Narendra Modi would always reinforce in our discussions, needed to also deliver improved living standards for all of India's population. From my perspective, this was a key benchmark for the success of the Australia–India project. Such goals cannot be achieved without promoting a stable, free and open Indo–Pacific. In other words, the developing world's economic goals are aligned with the developed world's security goals.

For this reason, the success that Prime Minster Modi and I achieved in elevating our bilateral relationship to a Comprehensive Strategic Partnership in June 2020 was more than a rhetorical accomplishment. It was backed up by a broad agenda of activity in almost every sphere of possible engagement. Our bilateral defence, security, economic, scientific, cultural, humanitarian and people-to-people ties were all expanded.

During the period 2020–21, we upgraded our defence cooperation through a new 2+2 ministerial dialogue and new agreements to facilitate sophisticated logistic cooperation, supporting our combined responsiveness to regional humanitarian disasters, and closer cooperation on defence science and technology. We put in place arrangements to improve regional cooperation on maritime shipping, disaster resilience and information sharing. In 2020, I was also pleased to rejoin Australia for the Malabar defence exercise with our Quad partners (India, the US and Japan) after a prolonged absence under previous governments. This would see our navies work together once again in highly sophisticated training exercises, from air defence and anti-submarine exercises to at-sea replenishment between ships.

We negotiated and signed our first-ever trade agreement with India, the Australia–India Economic Cooperation and Trade Agreement (ECTA) in April 2022, which eliminated tariffs on over 85 per cent of Australian exports to India, from wool, lamb and barley to critical minerals, non-ferrous metals and titanium dioxide, with reductions in many other sectors. Australia's manufacturers, processors and consumers also benefit from the elimination of tariffs on imports of Indian goods and inputs.

We concluded new agreements on critical and emerging technologies, including on cyber technologies, focusing on cyber governance, cyber security, capacity building, cybercrime and the digital economy. This also included support to establish the India–Australia Centre of Excellence for Critical and Emerging Technology Policy in Bengaluru in 2021.

We understood the important role India would play in building new and more resilient supply chains for critical minerals and rare-earths in the Indo–Pacific, and established the India–Australia Critical Minerals Research Partnership in 2023. This programme was designed to add value to Australian resource exports, work with India to prove up and commercialize critical minerals technology, and connect Indian mining companies with Australian mining equipment, technology and services companies to provide solutions, including technical and operational support, through our Global Mining Challenge programme.

In 2023, we established the India–Australia Innovation and Technology Challenge to tackle environmental and economic challenges together, such as waste reduction, water security and food system resilience, by supporting small businesses and entrepreneurs to launch innovative technology solutions. Back in 2021, our India–Australia Green Steel Partnership was established to develop and demonstrate technologies for steel decarbonization, including through the use of hydrogen, carbon capture and storage, and biomass, and we initiated a new energy dialogue with India to chart a shared path on energy transition in our economies.

In 2023, the world, and especially Australia, came together and celebrated India's successful moon landing. While serving as Prime Minister, I ensured Australia provided ongoing support to India's Gaganyaan space programme and established a dedicated India stream in the Australian Space Agency's International Space Investment initiative.

The same year, our new comprehensive partnership also established new Maitri programmes, including scholarships for high-achieving Indian students to study at Australian universities, a grants and fellowships programme to build links between our future leaders and support mid-career Australians and professionals to collaborate on strategic research and shared priorities, and a cultural partnership to boost the role of creative industries in our economic and people-to-people ties.

I was pleased that, together with Prime Minister Modi, we were able to take the Australia–India relationship to new heights during these important years. It demonstrated just what could be achieved when two diverse, multicultural democracies joined in a spirit of trust and understanding. It demonstrates what we can achieve when we make the effort as partners to look at the world and our shared challenges through each other's eyes.

Our partnership was not limited to our bilateral activity. Our regular alignment, during my time as Prime Minister with Prime Minister Modi, joined Australia and India together in multilateral fora to have a positive impact on promoting stability in the Indo–Pacific. This was particularly the case when we served together as founding members of the Quad Leaders' Summit with Japanese Prime Minister Yoshihide Suga and US President Joe Biden. This alignment also extended to our participation in the East Asia Summit, the G20, G7+ Dialogue, and the Asia–Pacific Economic Cooperation forum.

This alignment was built on our shared understanding that the Indo–Pacific is the region that will principally shape our prosperity, security and destiny—individually and collectively. It is a dynamic and diverse region, full of promise. But we are also not blind to the geopolitical realities. The Indo–Pacific is the epicentre of strategic competition. Tensions over territorial claims are growing. Military modernization is happening at an unprecedented rate. Democratic, sovereign nations are being threatened by foreign interference. Cyberattacks are becoming more sophisticated and frequent. Economic coercion is being employed as a tool of statecraft. Liberal rules and norms are under assault.

Together with Prime Minister Modi, I was pleased that Australia and India were able to seize new opportunities to create a more durable strategic balance in the Indo–Pacific, and, importantly, one that favours freedom. Together we were clear about our vision of a free, open and prosperous Indo–Pacific, underpinned by rules and respect for sovereignty. And we acted to defend and shape it, building economic capability, promoting maritime security, advocating regional cooperation, and working together to combat the global COVID-19 pandemic.

PARTNERS, *NATURALLY*

Australia sees India as a natural partner in shaping the future of the Indo–Pacific. It is about more than geography. It is history and values, our growing economic security, people-to-people ties, and our strong sense of mutual obligation. Building new habits and modes of cooperation and partnership are important.

We have also looked on with admiration as India has taken an increasingly active role in the Indo–Pacific and global affairs. I saw this on display when I had the great fortune to follow Prime Minister Modi at the COP26 Summit in Glasgow, where we were both presenting our national statements and sharing a platform with UK Prime Minister Boris Johnson in one of the leaders' sessions. Prime Minister Modi's points were well-made. I made similar points. The plan for a global net-zero emissions economy must enable developing economies to succeed, not stymie them.

When you look through an Indian lens, as the Raisina Dialogue teaches us to do, you can see why we need to rethink how we are addressing many global challenges, including the impacts of climate change. My observation is that too many approaches to addressing global challenges tend to be designed from a developed world mindset, without enough appreciation of the competing priorities and complexities faced by developing countries. This is a point Prime Minster Modi makes relentlessly in global forums.

The Western developed world demands action on climate change out of moral urgency but often struggles to reconcile this with the moral obligation of leaders in the developing world to deal with the immediate challenge to raise living standards for their people. The comfort of longer-term climate stability is no relief to the immediate deprivation and atrocious health outcomes that accompany poverty in developing countries. If climate solutions do not work in India, Indonesia and China, the global climate objective will not be achieved, regardless of what Western developed economies do. It must work in both worlds. The inclusive economic growth ambitions of developing countries must be achieved concurrently with global climate objectives.

This means more focus on technology, engineering and economics rather than political gestures or compensation hand-outs to—or demanding impractical regulations from—developing economies that inhibit their growth and prosperity, requiring them to settle for less. Developing countries prefer the sovereignty of sustainable prosperity to the economic dependency on Western compensation or Chinese debt diplomacy. These are just other forms of colonialism that many developing countries (including India) have spent lifetimes shaking off.

This means finding technological solutions for a net-zero economy that are focused on achieving viable commercial applications that will work at scale in developing countries, in places such as Gujarat rather than just in Bavaria or California. Such solutions must present a genuine alternative to traditional fossil fuels-based alternatives on a like-for-like basis. That means free of subsidies or tax concessions that developing countries do not have the resources to support in the same way developed countries do. It also requires maturity to understand that until such solutions are in place, transitions to the next-best lower emissions (but affordable and commercially viable) technologies must be embraced.

This is just one example of how adopting a 'Raisina

perspective' enables us to gain new insights into dealing with global, regional and bilateral challenges.

Another is how to attract private capital to realize and harness the economic potential of developing countries such as India, and the Global South more broadly, in building new, alternative and more resilient supply chains. A key priority already identified in Australia's own engagement with India is in energy and critical technology solutions that will dominate the global economy in the years ahead. The bottom line, literally, is that these investments must work and provide competitive returns to alternative investments. Failure to find solutions that work in developing countries for private capital will leave this task to governments and public capital, tilting the board in favour of more centralist, authoritarian regimes in the region. This risk highlights why regional security agendas cannot be restricted to defence cooperation alone but must practically embrace the promotion of economic sovereignty as a clear goal.

This is a topic for discussion at another time but one the Raisina Dialogue is well placed to lead, once again demonstrating the value of this important forum.

Section 3

New Opportunities: European Future
in the Indo-Pacific

Ursula von der Leyen

President of the European Commission

Terra Nova: Impassioned, Impatient, Imperilled

EVERY FIVE YEARS, WHEN INDIANS CAST THEIR VOTES IN parliamentary elections, the world watches with admiration as the world's largest democracy charts its future path, because the outcome of decisions made by 1.3 billion people resonates around the globe. This is especially true for Europe. As vibrant democracies, India and the European Union share fundamental values and common interests. Together, we believe in each country's right to determine its own destiny. Together, we believe in the rule of law and fundamental rights. And together, we believe that it is democracy that best delivers for citizens. So, despite our geographic distance and despite the different languages we speak, when we look at each other, we do not meet as strangers but as close friends. Democracy was born more than 2,000 years ago in Europe. But today, its largest home is India.

For the European Union, strengthening and energizing its partnership with India is a priority in this upcoming decade. Both our economies thrive in a world of common rules and fair competition. We share the same interests in safe trading routes, in seamless supply chains, and in a Free and Open Indo–Pacific. Both our regions are driving forces in the digital revolution. This makes us natural partners in setting global standards, to make sure that the rules of the analogue world also count in the digital domain. And of course, both India and the European Union are key in the transition to a more sustainable and green future for our planet. So, we must pool our strength in the fight against climate change. It is so urgent. This is our common responsibility not only towards the global community but also mostly towards the next generation.

AGGRAVATED AGGRESSIONS

However, our values are not shared by everyone. We all see the rising challenges to our open and free societies. This is true for the technological and the economic domain, but it is also true for security. The reality is that the core principles that underpin peace and security across the world are at stake, in Asia as well as in Europe. The images coming from Russia's attack on Ukraine have shocked and are shocking the whole world. In the April of 2022, I visited Bucha, the suburb of Kyiv which was devastated by Russian troops as they withdrew from the north of Ukraine. I saw with my own eyes the bodies lined up on the ground. I saw the mass graves. I listened to the survivors of atrocious crimes that the Kremlin's soldiers had committed. I saw the scars of bombed schools, resident houses and hospitals. These are severe violations of international law. Targeting and killing innocent civilians. Redrawing borders by force. Subjugating the will of a free people. The violence has only increased. This goes against the core principles enshrined in the UN Charter.

In Europe, we see Russia's aggression as a direct threat to our security. We will make sure that the unprovoked and unjustified aggression against Ukraine will be a strategic failure. This is why we are doing all we can to help Ukraine fight for its freedom. This is why we immediately imposed massive, sharp and effective sanctions. Sanctions are never a stand-alone solution. They are embedded in a broader strategy that has diplomatic and security elements. And this is why we have designed the sanctions in a way to sustain them over a longer period of time. Because this gives us leverage to achieve a diplomatic solution that will bring lasting peace. And we urge all members of the international community to support our efforts for lasting peace. And we must consider what it means for Europe and Asia that Russia and China have forged a seemingly unrestrained pact. They have declared that the friendship between them has 'no limits' and that there are 'no forbidden areas of cooperation'—this was in February this year. And then, the invasion of Ukraine followed. What can we expect from the 'new international relations' that both have called for?

This is a defining moment. Our decisions now will shape the decades to come. Our response to Russia's aggression today will decide the future of both the international system and the global economy. Will heinous devastation win or humanity prevail? Will the right of might dominate or the rule of law? Will there be constant conflict and struggle or a future of common prosperity and lasting peace? What happens in Ukraine will have an impact on the Indo–Pacific region. It already has. Countries battered by two years of the COVID-19 pandemic must deal now with rising prices for grain, energy and fertilizers as a direct result of Putin's war of choice. Thus, the outcome of the war will not only determine the future of Europe but also deeply affect the Indo–Pacific region and the rest of the world.

It is as important for the Indo–Pacific region as it is for Europe that borders are respected and that spheres of influence are rejected. We want a positive vision for a peaceful and prosperous Indo–Pacific region. The region is home to half of the world's population and 60 per cent of the global GDP. Our vision is that the Indo–Pacific region remains free and open and becomes more interconnected, prosperous, secure and resilient, with an open and rules-based security architecture that serves all interests. To this end, we will deepen our engagement with our partners in the region, including with ASEAN.

On China, we will continue to encourage Beijing to play its part in a peaceful and thriving Indo–Pacific region. The relationship between the European Union and China is simultaneously strategically important and challenging. All at once, China is a negotiating partner, an economic competitor, and a systemic rival. We will continue our multifaceted engagement, we will continue to cooperate on tackling common challenges, and we will protect our essential interests and promote our values.

On this foundation of engagement in the Indo–Pacific region, we seek to build a new common agenda for the twenty-first century. One major item on this agenda is the need, around the world, for massive investment to overcome the fallout of the COVID-19 pandemic and to modernize the economies. And as a consequence, some countries have been forced to take unsustainable offers. They face a situation where they do not fully control their own infrastructure—be it seaports or airports, be it bridges or railways. But investments in our future should never come at the expense of a country's independence. Throughout the 2020s, developing Asian countries will need to invest more than five per cent of their gross domestic product to meet the infrastructural needs of their own fast-growing economies. This means globally over US$1.7 trillion per year. The needs are massive, but so are the opportunities. This is why we have introduced Global Gateway. Global Gateway is Europe's vision for investment in clean and sustainable global infrastructure. Global Gateway will enable up to EUR 300 billion to support major infrastructure priorities around the world. From clean energy to digitalization, you name it, our offer will be transparent and values-driven. With Europe, what you see is what you get.

A DUAL AGENDA

Let me focus specifically on two points: first, on climate action. And here, let me take energy. Energy demand in India, for example, has doubled since 2000. And this is good news because it means better living conditions for millions of people. Over the next 20 years, India will need an additional energy capacity that is equal to the entire European energy consumption. So the question is, will this energy be clean? Or will it poison the air that we breathe? Will the energy be renewable and homegrown? Or will it increase our dependency and allow for blackmail in the future?

I was very glad to hear that Prime Minister Modi declared that India would be energy-independent before it celebrated the hundredth birthday of the country's independence, in 2047. The choices made today are crucial—not just for this great nation but also for the whole world. Global Gateway could bring, for example, to India and Bangladesh more hydropower produced in Nepal and Bhutan. It could build clean hydrogen infrastructure to power up their heavy industries. In 2022, I visited the headquarters of the International Solar Alliance. This is a great partnership launched by Prime Minister Modi and is now bringing together 86 countries. It is innovation at the service of people, as the International Solar Alliance will benefit most the least developed countries and the small island developing states.

Given the geopolitical and climate challenges we face, the business case today for solar is stronger than ever.

So we should massively scale it up—also through Global Gateway—for our common prosperity and for the benefit of the planet we all share. We can also help the climate when saving energy. I know this sounds obvious. But in a country the size of India, the sum of many small individual decisions can have a tremendous overall impact in the end. Just think of this example: as prices dropped dramatically in recent years, millions of Indians switched from using traditional old light bulbs to modern LED lighting technology. This resulted in annual energy savings of 30 terawatt-hours. This is roughly enough to power 28 million average Indian households for a year, or for the whole of Denmark, just through saving energy. There really is big-time potential in energy sufficiency and energy savings.

We also need to strengthen our cooperation in the digital field. This is my second point. Because cutting-edge technology is at the heart of our future cooperation, and Asia is a powerhouse when it comes to new technologies, from artificial intelligence to quantum computing. Our cooperation is about more than investment and infrastructure—it is about talent and technology based on fundamental values.

On standards, take this example: Today, India and the European Union both recognize that we are better off when we develop global standards for new technologies such as 5G, instead of seeking separate national solutions. And we share many of the same values when it comes to the digital world. We share the idea that privacy should be guaranteed online as well as offline and that technology should enhance individual freedom, not the state's ability to control us. Think about data protection. European companies outsource many of their IT processes to Indian companies. Europe generates almost one-third of the revenues for the Indian business process outsourcing sector. With equivalent rules, we could unlock even greater data flows between our regions, with immense benefits for the companies in our respective regions.

KEEPING FRIENDS CLOSE

As I mentioned earlier, for the European Union, the partnership with this region is one of our most important relationships for the coming decade, and strengthening this partnership is a priority. Our strategic cooperation should take place at the nexus of trade, trusted technology and security, notably in respect of challenges posed by rival governance models. And therefore, I was immensely pleased that two years ago, Prime Minister Modi and I agreed to establish an EU–India Trade and Technology Council to tackle key trade, economic and technological challenges. As like-minded partners, the European Union and India get to work on several tracks. We have launched negotiations on a free trade agreement as well as on investment protection and geographical indications. For Europe, this is a strategic investment in our partnership with India. The European Union is India's third most important trade partner. But we can do so much more. Our trade is far below our potential, both for Indian and European goods and services. So, this deal will bring new technologies, new investment, and unprecedented integration into shared value chains. We are the two largest democracies in the world, and together we have a lot to give for the benefit of the people.

We are indeed living in a Terra Nova, as the title of the 2022 Raisina Dialogue suggested. We all have to choose whether we want the Terra Nova to be a wild, dangerous and unliveable place, or a better home for all humankind. I am convinced that democracies will have a crucial role to play in defining the world of tomorrow. I want Europe to be a partner for Asia in shaping this new world. A world of independent yet interconnected countries. Working together for a more prosperous and peaceful world. Working together for the benefit of humankind.

This speech was delivered at the inaugural address at the 7th Raisina Dialogue, 2022 (25 April 2022).

Rosa Balfour and Zakaria Al Shmaly

Director, Carnegie Europe
Research Analyst, Carnegie Europe, and Doctoral
Fellow, United Nations University

Peripheral Vision: The European Union's Blind Spots in the Global South

HOW APPROPRIATE THE TERM 'GLOBAL SOUTH' IS, HAS become a hotly debated matter.[1] Merits and detractions around the definition aside, looking at the world from the perch of Brussels, the 'Global South' does provide one insight: it includes the parts of the world that the European Union (EU) has engaged with the least.

Europe's global footprint has been very slow in the making.[2] The EU's foreign policy has been overwhelmingly dealing with its so-called neighbourhood (Eastern Europe, North Africa and the Middle East). Its most important allies are in the transatlantic space, and it engages with the rest of the world mostly through specific prisms: trade and economics (from Canada to Vietnam, thus defying the Global South definition), the governance of common goods such as

---

[1]Sud, Nikita, and Diego Sánchez-Ancochea, 'Southern Discomfort: Interrogating the Category of the Global South', *Development and Change*, Vol. 53, No. 6, 2022, pp. 1123–50.

[2]Lehne, Stefan, and Francesco Siccardi, 'Where in the World is the EU Now?' *Carnegie Europe*, 2020, https://tinyurl.com/ywc5b5be. Accessed on 14 August 2024.

human rights and climate (through multilateral institutions, including working with the G77), and development policies (still the largest donor). All its dealings with the rest of the world, and much of the analysis of its global standing, also reveal that its self-perception as a force for good[3] often betrays mistaking itself for the world. As the Indian External Affairs Minister Dr S. Jaishankar noted, 'Europe has to grow out of the mindset that Europe's problems are the world's problems, but the world's problems are not Europe's problems.'[4]

Since 2022, when the United States and Europe struggled to get support against Russia's invasion of Ukraine, the EU has started its belated reckoning with the very different views coming from the Global South. And since Israel started waging a massive war on Gaza in retaliation for the terror attack of 7 October, the gap between the Global South, overwhelmingly supportive of the Palestinian cause, and the EU seemed never as wide.

This exercise needs to be placed in the context of a dynamic international order that is shifting and adjusting to the growing US–China rivalry and multipolarity. There are challenges and opportunities for the Global South, but also for Europe.

GAPS IN THE EU'S VISION

Without wanting to capture the kaleidoscope of views from the vast Global South—which vary across geography but also between government and society, urban and rural, as

[3]Balfour, Rosa, Lizza Bomassi, and Marta Martinelli, 'The Southern Mirror: Reflections on Europe from the Global South', *Carnegie Europe*, 2022, https://tinyurl.com/2cncchs4. Accessed on 14 August 2024.

[4]DeshGujaratHD, 'EAM S. Jaishankar Interacts at GLOBESEC in Slovakia; Full Video', *YouTube*, 2022, https://tinyurl.com/4seb8r2k. Accessed on 14 August 2024.

per exposure to international politics, as much as in any country[5]—the criticism the EU needs to reckon with can be clustered into a few categories. The 'double standards' accusation is very much related to international law and the EU's role in global war and peace. The EU's argument about Ukraine's sovereignty and territorial integrity was countered with criticism about the hypocrisy over the military interventions in Iraq (supported by most but not all EU member states) and Libya (UK and France). To an extent, it can be argued that the EU is guilty by association with those leading the military interventions, but the critique bears relevance even with respect to the different responses with regard to Ukraine when it was invaded by Russia in 2014 and Crimea when it was annexed, and again during the Russian invasion of Ukraine in 2022.[6] The hypocrisy accusation also pertains to inconsistencies towards international law when it comes to conflicts in the rest of the world.[7] The EU's mantra about the rules-based order and the global commons is also questioned as one that is perpetuating global inequality. During the COVID-19 pandemic, European states could access public debt in ways that lower-income countries could not, and prioritized European citizens in their vaccination policy.[8]

In trade and climate policies, the EU stands accused of pursuing extractive diplomacy to access raw materials

---

[5]Balfour, Bomassi, and Martinelli, 'The Southern Mirror: Reflections on Europe from the Global South'.

[6]Alden, Chris, 'The Global South and Russia's Invasion of Ukraine', *LSE Public Policy Review*, Vol. 3, No. 1, 2023, p. 16.

[7]Ambos, Kai, 'Ukraine and the Double Standards of the West', *Journal of International Criminal Justice*, Vol. 20, No. 4, 2022, pp. 875–92.

[8]Balfour, Rosa, Lizza Bomassi, and Marta Martinelli, 'Coronavirus and the Widening Global North-South Gap', *Carnegie Europe*, 2022, https://tinyurl.com/yyfhmk8d. Accessed on 14 Agust 2024.

or to raise environmental standards to the detriment of development.[9,10]

The EU's migration and asylum policy, and the contrast between the arrival of refugees from Syria and Afghanistan in 2015 and those from Ukraine since 2022—the different treatment of white Christian versus brown Muslim refugees—have attracted severe criticism about racialization and arbitrary boundary-creation. The EU border-control practices and its delegation to third parties, as exemplified in the infamous but not unique 2016 EU–Türkiye agreement[11] [12] that risks exacerbating rather than solving existing challenges, will not help the EU counter this negative perception.

All criticisms are coloured by post-colonial critiques that the EU as a whole has historically avoided addressing.[13] Looking forward, in light of the war, a shift towards the political right across Europe, and the promise to enlarge the EU and defend it against Russian aggression, a 'Fortress Europe' writ large is not an unrealistic scenario, but with even more securitized borders.

Some of these critiques are influenced by the ubiquitous narrative about geopolitical competition, which is shaped

---

[9]Bassey, Nnimmo, *To Cook a Continent: Destructive Extraction and Climate Crisis in Africa* Pambazuka, Cape Town, 2010.

[10]Lazard, Olivia, and Richard Youngs, 'The EU and Climate Security: Toward Ecological Diplomacy, Carnegie Europe', 2021, https://tinyurl.com/2ap9s87m. Acccessed on 14 August 2024.

[11]Adamson, Fiona B., and Kelly M. Greenhill, 'Deal-Making, Diplomacy and Transactional Forced Migration', *International Affairs*, Vol. 99, No. 2, 2023, pp. 707–25.

[12]Carrera, Sergio, and Andrew Geddes, 'The EU Pact on Migration and Asylum in Light of the United Nations Global Compact on Refugees: International Experiences on Containment and Mobility and Their Impacts on Trust and Rights', *European University Institute*, 2021, https://tinyurl.com/ms4uvwan. Accessed on 14 August 2024.

[13]Kundnani, Hans, *Eurowhiteness: Culture, Empire and Race in the European Project*, Hurst & Company, London, 2023.

more by the US and China than the EU; some are distorted by Russian and Chinese narratives about the corrupt West where liberal democracy is about to collapse. Post-colonial criticisms[14] are often manipulated by politicians from the Global South for populistic reasons.

To be sure, the EU needs to better understand these critiques to inform policy and make amends for the past. It also needs to think more creatively about working with partners to reform the international system, which is the origin of much of the problem of global inequality and its hubris.

Recent years have seen the EU and its member states engage more than ever with India. Instead of hectoring India to explicitly condemn Russia in the aftermath of the war and conditioning further cooperation on this basis, Europe paid attention to India's compulsions and concerns after New Delhi used its voice to not only speak for itself but also articulate what many other nations felt. In today's turbulent global context, the Raisina Dialogue, hosted by the Observer Research Foundation and India's Ministry of External Affairs, has been pivotal in addressing gaps in communication and understanding between nations.

It is an inescapable fact that addressing much of the world's problems requires global collaboration. Arguably, Europe has not yet lost the battle of narratives in the Global South[15] and can still offer a positive proposition that builds upon global commons in the interests of both partners.

---

[14]Giurlando, Philip, and Daniel F. Wajner, eds., *Populist Foreign Policy: Regional Perspectives of Populism in the International Scene*, Springer International Publishing, 2023.

[15]Dworkin, Anthony, 'Multilateral Development in Flux: Strengthening European Cooperation with the Global South', *European Council on Foreign Relations*, 22 November 2023, https://tinyurl.com/9hpedm9x. Accessed on 14 August 2024.

Looking beyond government policy and embracing societies would be a first step. Global public opinion, for instance, is less divided on Palestinian statehood than the policies of many governments. The values of liberal democracy are still cherished by many across the globe despite their governments. The pitted Global North versus Global South is often a construct exploited for political interest, or to hedge or divide among rivals.

Indeed, political leaders of the Global South too can be as transactionalist as they accuse the EU of being. Perhaps this could serve as a more pragmatic basis for relations. The recent Global Gateway Initiative—an initiative that supports infrastructure development worldwide—is seen as the EU's answer to China's Belt and Road Initiative. With an endowment of €300 billion (2021–27),[16] it may be belated and minimalist, but not too little, too late. The EU needs to be clear about its interests, acknowledge those of its partners, and pragmatically identify what added value a partnership with the EU would offer in terms of good governance, fighting climate change, and the economic benefits for both sides.

The EU also needs to build upon the positive perceptions that exist in the Global South among many citizens, democracy and human rights activists, business communities, academics and students, and many of those who have been engaged with EU programmes or representatives. Generously supporting the Loss and Damage Fund, as promised to the G77,[17] would boost the EU's image among global societies, not just governments. A more humane treatment of asylum seekers, such as that offered to Ukrainians, and a more liberal management of migration policy would alleviate pressure

---

[16]'Global Gateway', *European Commission*, https://tinyurl.com/atwbsyy4. Accessed on 14 August 2024.

[17]'COP28', *European Council*, https://tinyurl.com/4vbeb2u9. Accessed on 14 August 2024.

from border states, respect the dignity of asylum seekers, and reframe the EU's policy response in a constructive light in the Global South and amongst future European citizens.

Giorgia Meloni

Prime Minister of Italy

Provocation, Uncertainty, Turbulence: Lighthouse in the Tempest

IT IS AN HONOUR FOR ME TO INAUGURATE THIS YEAR'S Raisina Dialogue, and to do so in front of such an extraordinary audience. An audience that includes representatives from across the G20, with whom Italy shares a special responsibility to find solutions to our common global challenges. With this in mind, I would like to take this opportunity to share my appreciation for Prime Minister Modi's hard work on handling a complex presidency and to reiterate Italy's full support to its success.

I am told that the name of this international conference comes from Raisina Hill here in Delhi, from which the government is granted a broader view of India's capital city. In troubled times like today, this is, I think, a fitting metaphor for the vision that we, as leaders, thinkers, civil servants, need to adopt. It reminds me of the Palatino, the Campidoglio, and the other hills on which our ancestors founded ancient Rome, more than 2,000 years ago, from which an extensive network of roads connected different provinces, leading from the centre of the Italian peninsula to very diverse cultures. I think that it is also the way we need to do politics today. When I was running for the electoral campaign, I said that I did not want to climb the institutions to gain power, I wanted to climb the institutions for it is the only way that you can have a better view of what is happening and give the best solutions, and that is exactly what I see today.

As we look at events around us, our identity shapes our field of vision, both as individuals and as nations. Identity is shaped deeply by geography. At the same time, our thoughts could be shaped by provocation. Here, I would try to interpret in a positive way the very interesting question posed by the organizers of this conference, and I will start from the word 'provocation', which could certainly be considered as an affront to our sensitivities, but also as a spur to think in a different way. A challenge to accept the challenges of uncertainty and turbulence, for nothing is more certain than the uncertainty of our historic times: this is definitely the era of uncertainty, and at the same time, a period of unprecedented turbulence. We are in a tempest and we need to stand tall in considering our common challenges. We need to stand on the hill, take a deep breath, and see our lands and seas and their problems in a more enlightened way: we need a lighthouse in the storm. That is why opportunities like the Raisina Dialogue are so precious in times of accelerated and confusing events, which are at risk of being governed only with superficial thoughts and hasty actions.

Therefore, let us go back to the fundamental factors, including the geographical one, of our identities. And, considering some important similarities between the wide and profound wealth of the Indian and Italian ancient cultures and contemporary interests, I wonder if one can speak of the concept of 'peninsularity', which could have a place next to those of 'insularity' and 'continentality'.

Italy is deeply European. Our roots and history are European, and together with the nations across the continent, we have built Europe's identity through the centuries. Yet, all of Italy's long coastlines are bathed in the Mediterranean, the natural environment where the Judaic, Christian and Classic roots of Europe have developed. Geography has shaped our culture, our outward projection, and our growth as a civilization. And much like India, the 'peninsular factor' has given us a crucial resource: being both a continental and a maritime nation—a key advantage, making us natural platforms for trade, logistics, and the dissemination of culture and science.

For centuries, our maritime flows have looked towards the south and to the rest of the Mediterranean, which remains our natural neighbourhood and with whom we are continuing to build mutually beneficial relations. This is the spirit enshrined in our vision, also dubbed the 'Mattei Plan', for the Mediterranean and for all the African continent, with its growing population, challenges and opportunities. A vast region which has the resources, starting with energy, which are so crucial for Europe, but which should, first of all, benefit the peoples who are the owners of these commodities.

Our objectives are simple: ensuring prosperity, peace and lasting friendship through collaboration on an equal footing. A collaboration aimed at providing tangible benefits for all. Without predatory ambitions. Without coercion, economic or otherwise. In these first few months of my tenure, I gave priority to developing equal partnerships on common priorities such as energy, and Italy is working to be the bridge connecting the Eastern Mediterranean, Africa and Europe. Producer countries should benefit from their resources for their own prosperity and stability. Green energy, hydrogen and electricity will more and more be locally produced, for their own citizens and for Europe. Much like the energy transition, the digital transition is also based on connectivity. Data are the energy of our digital societies, and they will flow from India to Europe across the Mediterranean and Italy: the Blue Raman Project will link the Indo–Pacific to our European economies.

In the past, the Alps at our north protected Italy, but they were also the area of connection to the rest of Europe. Likewise, the Mediterranean Sea was for centuries a sort of blind alley, the extreme appendix of the Atlantic Ocean. Human progress and ingenuity, however, made the impossible possible: a change in geography, a passage from the Mediterranean to the Indo–Pacific, through the Suez Canal. Today, the Mediterranean is really the sea in the middle, the basin which stands between the two major maritime spaces of the globe: the Atlantic and the Indo–Pacific. Italy, with its peninsula, which lies in the very centre of the Mediterranean Sea, continues to be, in every way, a fully integrated part of the Euro–Atlantic community and of the cultural and political West, but it is more and more projected towards the Indo–Pacific, regaining the history of our maritime republics and of Marco Polo. Especially after the opening of the Suez Canal, the laws of physics, starting with the communicating vessels, are those of trade.

The impacts of such a shift are hard to exaggerate. Nearly 150 years later, as the Indo–Pacific has become a crucial centre of gravity for the global economy, 40 per cent of the EU's foreign trade passes through the South China Sea, and much more transits through the Indian Ocean.

Our two regions are more interconnected than ever before. Together, we account for 70 per cent of global trade, and the EU has become the biggest investor in the Indo–Pacific, which contributes to two-thirds of global economic growth.

The world's oceans connect us. They are essential to global commerce and our way of life. Today, shipping makes up 90 per cent of all international trade, and freedom of navigation is crucial for our economies.

Global interconnection has enabled our economies to cooperate and flourish, but it comes at a cost, especially in times of turbulence within the international community. What happens in Europe affects the Indo–Pacific in ways it would not have in the past. And what happens in the Indo–Pacific has direct repercussions in Europe. This is not a surprise, this is not a 'Black Swan'; it is rather a 'Gray Rhino' we should have seen, and it is something we need to keep in mind as we move forward. This implies a new approach on how we work together. We need to see the world through a progressive lens, to focus with the same level of attention on both long- and short-term dynamics. We face a war of aggression which brings us back to the tragedies of the twentieth century, but at the same time, we need to have the necessary vision to be prepared for the challenges of the twenty-first century.

The COVID-19 pandemic shook the foundations of international trade and mobility and exposed profound weaknesses in the resilience of global supply chains and in globalization as we knew it. They said we could solve every problem with free trade, that we were going to have democracy and richness for everybody; it was not like that, and we have to face what we were wrong in. As we worked to overcome these challenges, recover from the pandemic's devastating impacts, and restore global trade flows, the Russian war of aggression against Ukraine disrupted global energy prices, endangered food security, and sent waves of inflation across the world, to the detriment of the most vulnerable, especially in the Global South.

It also put at risk global stability, peace and security, which depend on a predictable, rules-based international order.

Just one year ago, we were poised to face the challenges

of the twenty-first century: eradicating poverty; addressing climate change; managing the impacts of digitalization on information flows and on daily life in our societies; and handling the advent of new technologies such as quantum computing and artificial intelligence.

However, the events of February 24th last year brought us back to the wars of the twentieth century.

I was in Kyiv last week. I witnessed the hard reality on the ground and felt the strength of the Ukrainians' national spirit among the destruction.

This is a war in Europe. Distant geographically from many other parts of the world, which in many cases are facing their own hardships closer at hand.

This should not, however, overshadow the relevance of what is at stake. The Russian attack is not simply an act of war or a localized conflict. It is an attack against the territorial integrity of a sovereign nation, in violation of the fundamental principles of the global order that enables the international community to thrive. We cannot allow the very foundations of international law to be threatened, without which only military force would be taken into account and every state in the world would risk being invaded by its neighbour. These are not only the interests of the European countries; these are the common goods for the coexistence of all countries of the world.

We cannot sit idly in the face of this provocation against the heart of the UN Charter, threatening to undermine stability across the globe. We cannot allow the law of the strongest to overcome the strength of the law.

I know that there are many who feel that Europe has, in the past, failed to acknowledge that the world's problems are also its own. And perhaps, until the past few years, our geopolitical stance has been less vocal than it could have been. This is no longer the case, and initiatives such as the

EU Strategy for the Indo–Pacific demonstrate that our views have, indeed, broadened. Regional affairs rapidly turn into global affairs in today's interconnected world. And unfortunately, Europe's problem today has become the world's problem. Italy and India share a profound conviction. That only the rule of law can allow humanity to prosper and develop, in balance and harmony. As forward-looking countries, with rich cultures dating back millennia, we have a common, human-centric vision in which democracy, science, peace and prosperity go hand in hand. The relationship between artificial intelligence and ethics is crucial: all developments must be human-centred. Our strength lies in our human capital, in our abilities to create and to push the boundaries of science, knowledge and technology, while keeping the state at the service of our citizens. We are building new bridges between academic and research centres of Italy and India.

Despite the long history of our respective people, we are both young as states. We have had to overcome intense, similar struggles to establish ourselves as independent states. It is no coincidence that the Italian 'Risorgimento' was among the sources of inspiration for many Indians fighting for their independence, and that the work of Giuseppe Mazzini, a key figure for Italy's unification, was translated, read, and studied by many Indian patriots. Gandhi himself, whose *Young India* drew from Mazzini's 'Giovine Italia', recognized his influence, saying: 'There are few examples in the world of a man who, alone, accomplished his country's resurrection by the power of his thoughts and extreme dedication, throughout the course of his life.' Our civilizations have met, touched, and influenced each other along the centuries. There are many examples, but one struck a particular chord with me: the discovery of an Indian ivory statue in the 2,000-year-old ruins of Pompeii. A powerful testimony to the depth of our historical relations.

Our cultures are hymns to life and love, and we will continue to fight, with determination, against those who worship hate and violence. Terrorism is a cancer that also needs to be faced through wide international cooperation and it must be addressed with leadership and resolve.

As I sit in my office in Palazzo Chigi in Rome, which is known as the 'prua d'Italia', the bow of Italy, I am often reminded of my nation's maritime nature. As we navigate the waters of the world, we must navigate the new horizons of the twenty-first century. We need to see better as we move through uncertainty, to strengthen the resilience of our global relationships through greater cooperation and diversification.

It is true that, as the title of this year's Raisina Dialogue reminds us, we are weathering a storm. A terrible storm, which is making it difficult for our ships to sail, through cross-winds and violent waves crashing on the surf. Fear has crept into their crews, and even the most seasoned sailors are hard-pressed to make the right decisions. Those who are at the stern, carrying the responsibility of their crews and of their ships, can make the difference. This is precisely the choice we, as leaders, have ahead of us: either swaying into turbulent waters or guiding our ships towards the safety of a friendly harbour. Our compass is our common endeavour to protect the shared human values that form the basis of our coexistence.

India is a key player in this broad landscape, bathing in the Indo–Pacific, much as Italy is at the heart of the Mediterranean, and our two countries have important contributions to make together. This is why Prime Minister Modi and I have just announced the scaling up of our bilateral relations to a Strategic Partnership.

Building on bilateral tools and broader programmes such as the EU Global Gateway, Europe and the Indo–Pacific—but also Latin America and the African continent—are enhancing their collaboration on all fronts, from connectivity to infrastructure and fair and sustainable trade, while keeping in mind a strategic priority for all of us: the energy transition.

This will be a key element in the global fight against climate change, to which we all need to contribute, with different tasks and responsibilities. We have to do it bearing in mind our responsibilities towards the future generations but also to our citizens today, and we need to do it in a balanced way: each country has to do its part. Failing to do so would have profound impacts on humanity worldwide, directly through food shortages, droughts, extreme weather events, and other disasters, but also indirectly, through new conflicts arising from climate-induced migrations and transboundary disputes over scarce resources.

The need to accelerate the energy transition has been compounded by the energy crisis, which has highlighted the vulnerability of economies across the world. It has, however, also shown that global coordination on climate change is not a zero-sum-game but a true shared interest. The same is true for technological development and dissemination, where India and countries throughout the Indo–Pacific have a central role to play, given their highly skilled workforce, their resources, and their strategic position along the global value chains.

Our ability to work together on renewable energy, green hydrogen, circularity, and the twin transitions will determine our success. And it requires a functioning international order.

This is something that we humans of the twenty-first century cannot do without and that we need to nurture and reaffirm at every turn. The governance of multilateral organizations must be updated. But the cornerstones of multilateralism cannot be called into question, as they are also the cornerstones of peace and freedom.

Let us not feed the false metaphor of a world divided—the West against the rest. The unshakable unity in the face of the growing threat to international peace and stability goes well beyond the Western interest; it is a common interest. This is, I believe, a key message that could emerge from the Indian G20 presidency as well as from the Raisina Dialogue. A message of hope, a message of unity.

Every nation can be a lighthouse, with the wealth and pride of its tradition and identity, which some would like to forget or hide or kick, but we are nothing without our roots. Our rights and the capability we have to recognize them depend on our tradition. Those who want to kick our tradition and our identity want to kick our rights, so it is an important struggle that we are facing all over the world, and I know that on this, we have the same point of view. Lighthouses do not obscure each other, but they can shine together and help all of us navigate these troubled waters.

Thank you very much.

This speech was delivered at the inaugural address at the 8th Raisina Dialogue, 2023 (2 March 2023).

Mette Frederiksen

Prime Minister of Denmark

Charting Green Frontiers: India and Denmark as Strategic Allies

TODAY THE WORLD IS FACING COMPLEX AND OVERLAPPING crises within areas ranging from climate and environment to food, health, energy and outright military conflict. Crises that reinforce one another and cause instability and insecurity across borders and regions. They affect our supply chains. They challenge our security and our way of life. Security is no longer merely about making our communities safe from traditional threats, but increasingly about dealing with new and interconnected challenges.

From the Indo–Pacific to the Atlantic and beyond, our security is closely linked. Russia's illegal war of aggression against Ukraine is not just about European security. It affects people and countries across the world through increased food and energy insecurity, inflation, and a weakening of international rules and norms. The war has highlighted the adverse effects of our interconnected world. However, it would be wrong to turn inwards in response or to shy away from our fundamental belief in the benefits of an open, engaging world. Rather, we need to take the necessary precautions to ensure that we can continue engaging with each other in an inclusive and trustful manner. While remaining committed to the rules-based multilateral system, we need to consider both economic and security interests.

The latter will require us to diversify supply chains, ensure control of sensitive technologies, and forge new partnerships while strengthening old ones. This cannot be successfully undertaken by any one nation on its own. It can only be achieved through collective efforts.

There is a need for a reinvigorated commitment by all stakeholders to tackle our global challenges together and to renew our collaboration in defence of international rules and norms. Being fortunate enough to have addressed the Raisina Dialogue, I can personally attest to the value of the forum, which throughout the last decade has provided an outstanding platform for reflections and consultations on global challenges.

A MATCH FOR A GREENER FUTURE

Our generation's greatest challenge is the climate crisis. It will require a new level of global cooperation between governments, businesses, civil society and individuals if we are to achieve the climate and Sustainable Development Goals we have agreed on. It is a daunting task, but nonetheless one we need to address head-on. The alternative is societal, economic, security and environmental consequences on a scale difficult to imagine but which we unfortunately are already experiencing.

In 2020, India and Denmark signed a Green Strategic Partnership, the first of its kind for both nations. It is a mutually beneficial partnership to advance political cooperation, expand economic relations and green growth, create jobs, and strengthen cooperation in addressing global challenges and opportunities. The Green Strategic Partnership builds on a whole-of-government approach involving a range of sectors: climate, energy, environment, water, sustainable and smart cities, food and agriculture, science and innovation, green shipping, labour mobility, health, digitization and culture. The partnership sets the framework for cooperation on green transition in a number of areas, with energy cooperation and sustainable water management as central pillars.

India has high green ambitions in the field of energy transition, while also experiencing some of the world's highest growth rates. Denmark has long been a global frontrunner in green and renewable energy and demonstrated that it is possible to commit strongly to a green trajectory while at the same time creating growth and employment. Experts from the Danish Energy Agency are embedded in organizations under the Indian Ministry of New and Renewable Energy and the Ministry of Power, where they contribute to make a green difference every single day. Here, they support India in its ambitious goal of becoming climate neutral by 2070 by contributing to developing offshore wind policies and integrating renewable energy into the Indian power system. Furthermore, water experts from the Danish Environmental Protection Agency, Danish water utility companies, and the City of Aarhus are working with Indian stakeholders to support India's initiatives to address the enormous challenges in the Indian water sector, by utilizing Danish know-how and technology.

The Green Strategic Partnership has already shown concrete results. One example is the India–Denmark Energy Partnership, which focuses on capacity building and technology transfer in the areas of offshore wind, energy modelling, and integration of renewable energy. Through this partnership, the Danish–Indian Centre of Excellence on Offshore Wind and Renewable Energy has been created with an aim to contribute to the tender of up to 37 gigawatts of offshore wind power in India by 2030. Denmark is also assisting India with know-how and skills in its ambitious

Jal Jeevan Mission, in the process providing clean water to nearly 200 million households in the countryside. The Green Strategic Partnership is an example of how we can achieve results by pooling resources and leading by example. This can hopefully serve as an inspiration to others. It shows how growth and the green transition are not mutually exclusive, but can go hand in hand. India and Denmark have partnered up in the journey towards a greener world. Our two nations may, at first glance, look like an odd match, but the partnership is unique in combining our different capabilities. Denmark is a country of less than six million inhabitants. India is a country of 1.4 billion people—now the most populous country in the world. Denmark makes up just 0.4 per cent of the global economy, but has highly specialized skills within certain fields. India, on the other hand, is one of the world's largest economies on course to more than doubling its share of global GDP by 2050. It is an ambitious partnership that matches skills with scale, as Indian Prime Minister Narendra Modi himself eloquently put it.

THE IMPORTANCE OF PARTNERSHIPS AND GLOBAL COOPERATION

The Green Strategic Partnership between India and Denmark also seeks to have a global impact by aiming at delivering on the 2030 Agenda for Sustainable Development and the Paris Agreement. As a part of the partnership, India and Denmark collaborate in the International Solar Alliance, and during the Indian presidency of the G20, Denmark has participated in working groups on climate and environment and energy transition. Thus, we hope to apply the experience gained from our close bilateral relationship globally. India and Denmark also share ambitions on increasing global mobilization of climate finance. This will require close collaboration, both in order to raise the necessary private capital and to pursue ambitious reforms of the international financial architecture, including the multilateral development banks, to ensure it delivers for all.

On another front, partnerships also play a crucial role in making our societies more secure and robust. This became apparent to all when COVID-19 tested the capacity of healthcare systems across the globe. The many negative consequences of Russia's illegal war against Ukraine have likewise underscored how trade and interdependencies can also bring risks and vulnerabilities. The lesson from an old story by the famous Danish author Hans Christian Andersen still applies: It is unwise to put all your eggs in one basket. That is why Denmark has supported new EU industrial policy measures in order to reduce critical dependencies and build resilience by diversifying supply chains and investing in research and innovation. However, if we truly want to ensure our influence on the technologies of tomorrow, we need to form new partnerships as well as expand existing ones. The India–EU Trade and Technology Council, only the second of its kind, stands as a prominent example of how we forge bonds in new and emerging fields for the mutual benefit of all partners.

It is my firm belief that global development, peace and prosperity are contingent on mutually beneficial partnerships and cooperation based on equality. We must become better at listening to each other. As Prime Minister Modi said in the context of India's G20 presidency, one world does not equal one philosophy. India has for decades lived by this ethos, serving as a central voice for the Global South while upholding diversity and rejecting one-size-fits-all models of national development. India has shown that it is willing to walk the talk as a *vishvaguru* (a world teacher or world leader), as when the COVID-19 pandemic swept across the world, India supplied and donated tens of millions of vaccine doses to the world. I firmly believe this kind of inclusive leadership will be crucial to solving the many global challenges we are facing.

India's respect for diversity and differences is also reflected in Denmark's own commitment to multilateral cooperation, and in our belief that sustainable development can only be achieved by working together on the basis of mutual respect and dialogue. As a small country with a strong democratic tradition, Denmark understands the value of an international order where all countries—large and small—have an equal voice. To that end, Denmark is a strong proponent of a more inclusive and effective multilateral system able to address the global challenges we face. Solidarity and cross-regional cooperation are at the heart of our international and multilateral engagement. These are values we hope to further promote if Denmark is elected to serve on the UN Security Council in 2025–26.

The Danish Government remains fully committed to developing partnerships as a way of solving our common problems. Today Denmark has established green strategic partnerships or energy collaboration agreements with countries responsible for 70 per cent of the world's CO_2 emissions. I am certain that the Raisina Dialogue in a similar spirit will continue to provide an excellent platform for promoting new and closer partnerships, while serving as a space for highlighting challenges to our mutual development, and sharing valuable experiences on how to solve them, for the benefit of all humankind.

Section 4

Guards of Honour: Forging a
More Secure World

Benjamin Netanyahu

Prime Minister of Israel

Managing Disruptive Transitions: Ideas, Institutions, and Idioms

NAMASTE. PRIME MINISTER MODI, MY DEAR FRIEND, ISRAEL'S dear friend, thank you on behalf of the people of Israel for the exceptional welcome that you are giving us and the opportunity to address this forum with the distinguished guests that are here from so many nations, from India and from Israel. Thank you for this unbelievably moving visit and thank you for the opportunity also to address the challenges that face us in the future and how together we can work to achieve prosperity, security and peace.

I want to tell you first how we in Israel overcame our challenge. We are a tiny people, live in a small country, somewhat smaller than India, a lot smaller than India, no natural resources, no great rivers. Well, the Jordan is a great river, but it is a stream, it trickles. And yet, we have become, I think, a force to contend with on the world scene, and I would like to describe to you the process that we went through and then discuss what we could do together.

I was thinking about the journey that we made yesterday in that magnificent ceremony in the President's house, and I was thinking that 75 years ago, our people were like a wind-tossed leaf. A third of our people were destroyed in heaps of ashes, and yet, there I was, standing and representing the Jewish people in the great nation of

India, one of the great powers on earth. What led to this transformation?

It was our understanding of the principal lesson of Jewish history and also a simple lesson in our turbulent region, and it is this: the weak do not survive. The strong survive. You make peace with the strong. You make alliances with the strong. You are able to maintain peace by being strong, and therefore, the first requirement of Israel from the time of our first Prime Minister David Ben-Gurion was to achieve the minimal strength that is required to assure our existence. Now, what is the source of strength? Various questions arise about what is the nature of power.

There is soft power. There is hard power. I like soft power. Hard power is often better. What does it mean? What does it mean to have power? Well, the first prerequisite is military power. You need F35s, you need submarines, you need interceptors, you need cyber, you need intelligence. In the case of Israel, you need a lot of intelligence to compensate for our size. There is one thing that characterizes all the things that I just mentioned. They cost money, a lot of money, and as time goes by, they cost more and more money. So defence—the prerequisite of security, and security always comes first—costs a great deal of money, as does education, as does health, as does infrastructure—all the requirements that our people justly deserve once we provide security.

Where does the money come from? It comes from the second source of power. That is, economic power. I view the requirements of providing, of securing our future, as dependent on three sources of power—military power and now economic power. How do you get economic power? Surely you need education. Prime Minister Modi and I were talking about how we educate our youth. In the case of Israel, there is one big education machine. It is called the Israeli Defence Force, and everyone comes in and we give training, we give technology, we give an assessment, an understanding of the main techniques of technology that are important for the future, also for civilian future.

And yet, we have seen other societies that have had educated people, highly educated people, extraordinary mathematicians, physicists, metallurgists, that did not achieve economic power. In fact, they collapsed. I am talking about the former Soviet Union. But if you took, in Soviet times, if you took one of those mathematicians and speared him or her away to California, to Silicon Valley, they would be producing value within two weeks, because the requirement— the necessary requirement for the development of technology, innovation, ingenuity—the necessary requirement are free markets or freer markets. Technology and value added is produced by firms. Firms produce technology. They perfect it, they multiply it, they re-invent. Firms are critical, and therefore, the technology, the policy that produces growth and gives you competitive advantage is the economic policy that makes it possible for firms to do business. It is called being business-friendly.

I have to say that I was absolutely astounded when I learned yesterday that Prime Minister Modi has moved India on the scale of the ease of doing business 42 places in three years. Prime Minister Modi understands exactly what I am talking about. In other words, if you want to have economic power, you must reduce taxes, simplify taxes, and you must cut bureaucracy. Government can facilitate economic growth. Government can block economic growth. In our cases, Israel and India, we don't have any bureaucracy to contend with. You know that. So, a main job of the leaders of both India and Israel is to reduce this bureaucracy, to cut it, as I call it, with a machete, with an axe, so that the firms can go on with their business of doing business. This gives strength. We have done this in Israel. We have transformed an economy that was very centralized and very bureaucratized into a free market economy that allows the technological genius of our people and our young people to flower.

This is what starts the startups. Startups are made by young people, thousands of them. The minute we created this climate, this climate of creativity and entrepreneurship, the talents break forth. I believe that this second power is critical to the first. I believe that the growth of military power and military influence is dependent ultimately on economic power, and economic power also facilitates all the elements of life that we need.

We have achieved that transition to a more liberal economy and we are absolutely committed to continuing on this path because we know we are in a never-ending race. The exponential growth that you talked about is achieved today by the confluence of Big Data, connectivity, and artificial intelligence. The countries that will seize the future are those that will innovate along these lines. The future belongs to those who innovate. Those who innovate will innovate in freer market terms. And this is what we all must do. We are doing it. India is doing it.

Now, having established our military power and our economic power, we are developing our third power, and the third power is political power. By political power, I mean the ability to make political alliances and relationships with many other countries. In the last year alone, I visited six continents; Asia, Africa, Europe—Africa I visited three times in 18 months—South America and of course North America, and Australia, so all six. And we have a growing number of countries with whom we have trade relations, cultural relations, technological relations, security relations. This is very important for us in order to broaden our position in the world, in order to have the kind of relations that ultimately secure your future. Military power. Economic power. Political power.

But there is, I believe, a fourth power, and it is the power of our values, of our traditions. I was asked by African leaders, I was asked in a symposium in the UN, about Israeli technologies that are helping change Africa. I was asked: What is the secret of Israel? You know, we create a lot of problems in Africa, he said, and you come and you create solutions with us. What is your secret? You are such a small country. How do you do this? And I said: Look, we are a special people. We are like a tree that has deep roots in our ancient soil, our ancient tradition, and yet we throw up leaves to the heavens. We keep searching, keep inquiring, keep looking for new ways. The branches go up to the sky and the roots are deep in the earth. I believe that this is the secret of Israel. I also believe it's the secret of India. It is exactly the same thing—powerful traditions, ancient cultures of which we are so deeply proud, and yet these inquiring minds also reach out to the sky, reach out for new solutions to the problems all the time, and I think this characterizes our two peoples.

But I believe too that there is one thing else that binds us together, and I think perhaps it is the most important of all. We have a special relationship. Among the many countries, we have a special relationship to democracies. India is the world's most populous democracy. It is a place that shows that humanity can be governed with freedom, that we can secure the rights of people, those things that make life worthwhile—the ability to think as we want; speak as we want; believe what we want, in a society that is pluralistic, diverse and free. This is what India is about. This is what Israel is about.

So, the fourth thing that binds us together is our values, and the most important value is the value of democracy.

Well, I believe that this is not merely a passing thing. We are now moving from a unipolar road to a multipolar road. We have an exceptional relationship with a democracy called the United States of America. We have an exceptional relationship with a democracy called Canada and other countries. The reason I mention the importance of democracies is because even though we have relations with most countries in the world, if we are to live in a world that protects international norms—something that you, Prime Minister Modi, talk about all the time—then we must have the ability to protect those norms, and democracies bind to each other, connect to each other in natural ways. We are, I think, naturally sympathetic to India. When I walk in the streets of India, as I just did in Agra, I saw the sympathy and friendship of people. Somebody said to me: We are so happy that you are friends with our Prime Minister and that he is friends with you. We are friends with you. We are friends with Israel. It is a natural friendship and natural partnership of democratic and free peoples.

Our way of life is being challenged. Most notably, the quest for modernity, the quest for innovation is being challenged by radical Islam and its terrorist offshoots from a variety of corners, and this can upset the international system. I think that one of the ways to overcome such a challenge is to strengthen the relationship between our two great democracies. The alliance of democracies, I think, is important to secure our common future. I believe that the possibilities are endless. We have discussed in this visit how we can strengthen our two nations in the civilian areas, in the security areas, in every area. It is something I look forward to do.

I want to thank you again for giving me this opportunity to bring India to Israel and Israel to India. Your historic visit broke ground. You are the first leader of India to come to Israel in 3,000 years. Let us hope it will not take long for your next visit. I know that. But I want to tell you how delighted we are in Israel. I want to tell you that we believe in India, as you believe in Israel. Good luck to India. Good luck to Israel, and may God bless the India–Israel alliance.

This speech was delivered at the inaugural address at the 3rd Raisina Dialogue, 2018 (16 January 2018).

Angus John Campbell and Greg Moriarty

Chief of the Defence Force of Australia
Secretary, Department of Defence of Australia

The India–Australia Defence and Security Partnership in 2024 and Beyond

INDIA IS A TOP-TIER SECURITY PARTNER FOR AUSTRALIA, and our nations have never been more strategically aligned. Our defence forces are undertaking more complex and frequent exercises to enhance interoperability, and have established a regular and growing pattern of strategic dialogues, training exchanges and senior-level visits.

This essay will explore our shared strategic circumstances, the importance of the Indian Ocean to Australia's security and prosperity, the centrality of India to Australia's Indo–Pacific strategy, and the future trajectory of the India–Australia defence and security partnership.

SHARED HISTORY

Our shared past links two of the world's oldest continuous civilizations, and includes our comradeship in two world wars. Indeed, 67 Australian soldiers lay at permanent rest on Indian soil to this day.

In 1915 at Gallipoli, Australians, New Zealanders and Indians fought side by side as part of the larger ill-fated Dardanelles Campaign. Facing the same bullets, artillery barrages and brutal conditions, a camaraderie sprang up between the troops. Indian soldiers shared chapattis with the men they came to know as 'Anzacs', and they, in turn, shared the biscuits sent to them by mothers and sweethearts, which we today call 'Anzac biscuits'. Just over 25 years later, Australian and Indian soldiers once again found themselves fighting together in North Africa and Southeast Asia. On the hills of Gallipoli, and in the desert and jungle of El Alamein and Burma, Australia and India built the foundations upon which our contemporary defence relationship rests.

The importance of India to Australia's national security has long been understood. While visiting India in 1950, Sir Robert Menzies, Australia's longest-serving prime minister, stated that developments in the world 'would be profoundly affected by what happens in India' and that our two nations should 'learn to think together and act together for the world's peace'. Seventy-three years later, Australia's current prime minister, Anthony Albanese, pledged to place India 'at the heart of Australia's approach to the Indo–Pacific and beyond' during his first official visit to the country.

Australia's relationship with India is not one of temporary or passing interest. It is deeply rooted in history. It is enduring. And it is increasing in importance. Particularly in response to our rapidly evolving security environment.

STRATEGIC CONTEXT

Our region, the Indo–Pacific, is the world's economic and strategic centre of gravity. It is home to more than half of the world's population, nearly two-thirds of the global economy, and seven of the world's largest militaries.

Military spending in the Indo–Pacific totalled US$575 billion in 2022. This amount was 2.7 per cent higher than that in 2021, and continues an upward trend observed since at least 1989.

Commensurate with this increased spending, a range of new military technologies are proliferating in our region across all domains, including long-range high-speed weapons, sophisticated sensors, autonomous systems, modern warships, and cutting-edge strike capabilities.

Technological disruptions and multiplying climate risks continue, and the prospect of state-on-state conflict is less remote than it once was. Additionally, the use of coercive statecraft, lawfare, and influence operations in the grey zone between peace and war undermines the traditional understandings of the international rules-based order and tests the thresholds for a conventional military response.

It is clear that we now live in an era and region of great power competition that may last for some time. These effects are not confined to the Western Pacific or maritime Southeast Asia. Indeed, the Indian Ocean is also the location of increasing geostrategic contestation.

AUSTRALIA'S LONG-STANDING INTEREST IN THE INDIAN OCEAN

As a trading nation, the Indian Ocean is extremely important to Australia's regional connectivity and economic security. Over half of Australia's seaborne exports leave Indian Ocean ports and five of Australia's top 15 trading partners—India, Indonesia, Malaysia, Singapore and Thailand—border the Indian Ocean. Australia possesses the longest Indian Ocean coastline and the region's largest search and rescue area. The Indian Ocean is also home to some of Australia's largest hydrocarbon deposits and important offshore territories, including the Cocos Keeling Islands.

Consequently, the Indian Ocean, particularly the

Northeast Indian Ocean, is central to Australia's prosperity and national security, a point articulated in Australia's *2020 Defence Strategic Update* and reaffirmed in the Australian Government's response to the more recent *Defence Strategic Review*.

As a resident power, it is only natural that Australia possesses an enduring interest in the Indian Ocean's future. But the nature of that future is increasingly unclear. The rapid expansion of military capabilities without adequate transparency, combined with actions taken by some actors to undermine and weaken the normative and legal structures that have enabled our region's prosperity, is generating significant uncertainty and anxiety.

AUSTRALIA'S VISION FOR OUR REGION

In response to our rapidly evolving strategic circumstances, Australia is focused on how it can best deploy its statecraft to preserve regional stability and prosperity while deterring conflict. As the hard power component of these efforts, the Australian Defence Force (ADF) has an important role to play in this regard. That is why Australia has commenced a multi-generational reinvestment in its defence capabilities to ensure the ADF is adequately equipped, structured, and postured so that it can constructively contribute to regional security, deter conflict, and maintain the capacity to operationally respond as directed by the Australian Government.

However, as a relatively modestly sized military, the ADF recognizes that it does not possess the capacity to support our region's peace and prosperity alone. Australia is always going to be stronger if it has partners who will work with it in common cause. This truth permeates Australia's national history and is absolutely central to our military and strategic cultural heritage.

Australia needs friends, and our friends need Australia. Together we are stronger, and the region is stronger. That is why the ADF is deepening its collaboration and integration with allies, partners, and like-minded friends for the common good of our region. And no partner is more important and consequential for Australia in the Indian Ocean than India.

GROWTH IN THE INDIA–AUSTRALIA DEFENCE AND SECURITY PARTNERSHIP

Australia and India share a deep and abiding interest in the security and stability of the Indo–Pacific and the norms and laws that govern the sea, particularly the United Nations Convention on the Law of the Sea, freedom of navigation, and unimpeded trade. As the pre-eminent maritime power in the Indian Ocean, India plays an essential leadership role.

Through the Quad, our nations have partnered with the US and Japan to advance a practical and positive agenda that supports an open, inclusive, and resilient Indo–Pacific. We are doing so by jointly responding to our region's most pressing challenges, including climate change, infrastructure, humanitarian assistance and disaster relief, and maritime security. The Quad complements other efforts by Australia and India to deepen regional engagement, including with the ASEAN, Pacific partners, and key Indian Ocean organizations, particularly the Indian Ocean Rim Association and the Indian Ocean Naval Symposium.

The signing of the India–Australia Comprehensive Strategic Partnership (CSP) in 2020 was a watershed moment in the history of our bilateral relationship, reflecting the extensive growth in relations across strategic, economic and cultural fields.

In the area of defence and security, the number and complexity of joint exercises and activities have increased significantly. In the maritime domain, our navies continue to strengthen warfighting capabilities through our premier bilateral maritime exercise, AUSINDEX. These training activities are augmented by other multinational naval exercises, including MILAN and KAKADU. Exercise MALABAR (which brings together the navies of India, Australia, Japan and the US) plays a particularly important role in advancing collaborative planning, interoperability, and the joint employment of advanced naval warfare tactics. Further naval engagements include the first deployment of Indian Navy and Air Force aircraft to Australia's Cocos Keeling Islands in June and July 2023 and the first visit of an Indian Navy submarine to Australia in August 2023.

On land, Exercise AUSTRAHIND continues to provide our armies an excellent opportunity to promote mutual understanding, share tactics, and develop interoperability.

In the air, exercises between the Royal Australian Air Force and Indian Air Force have continued to grow in intensity and sophistication. Exercise PITCH BLACK, in particular, has afforded unique and significant opportunities for our air forces to work together, conduct combat drills and undertake complex aerial scenarios. PITCH BLACK has also enabled our air forces to collaborate on logistics and sustainment, with personnel-sharing procedures for refuelling, munitions loading and base-support operations.

P-8 AIRCRAFT DEPLOYMENTS

The Mutual Logistics Support Arrangement, which sits beneath our CSP, has also played a critical role in paving the way for more sophisticated defence activities. For instance, it has been a critical enabler of the successful deployments of Indian Navy P-8I aircraft to Australia and of Royal Australian Air Force P-8A aircraft to India since 2022.

These deployments have been instrumental in enhancing our shared maritime domain awareness and are a clear demonstration of our joint commitment to supporting maritime security in the Indian Ocean in accordance with the United Nations Convention on the Law of the Sea.

AUSTRALIA'S EXPANDING MILITARY REPRESENTATION IN INDIA

Australia has also increased the level of its military representation in India, elevating its resident Defence Adviser in New Delhi to a one-star Head of Australian Defence Staff position. We are working to establish army and naval adviser positions in New Delhi, which will complement the existing air adviser position. The elevation of Australia's level of military representation to India clearly demonstrates the significant growth in our defence and security relationship and reaffirms Australia's commitment to further strengthening this important partnership.

DEFENCE INDUSTRY COOPERATION

Cooperation between Australia and India in the defence industry continues, underpinned by our Defence Science and Technology Implementing Arrangement. Enhanced industrial base cooperation offers the opportunity to increase the resilience of our respective supply chains, deliver enhanced capability to our forces, and increase defence interoperability. These efforts are supported by the Joint Working Group on Defence Industry Research and Material, which has now met twice since its reinvigoration in 2022.

PERSONNEL EXCHANGES

Senior visits and personnel exchanges continue at pace. The General Rawat India–Australia Young Defence Officers' Exchange Program, named in memory of India's inaugural Chief of Defence Staff, epitomizes this positive momentum. In honour of General Bipin Rawat's legacy, the exchange programme aims to expose young officers from Australia and India to each other's training philosophies and capabilities to strengthen our people-to-people links.

The first iteration of the exchange programme occurred in March 2023 and saw 15 ADF officers visit India. Australia looks forward to reciprocating by hosting Indian officers in 2024. This unique programme is an investment in our partnership and future, allowing our personnel to develop the high levels of familiarity and trust our growing partnership demands.

Fundamentally, the unprecedented growth in our bilateral defence and security partnership is a testament to the extraordinary efforts of our people—their vision, hard work, patience and commitment. It is also a clear demonstration of the trust and deep bonds of affection that exist between our two nations.

In a more contested world, those countries that are able to integrate their resources and combine their strengths will have a competitive advantage. Australia's partnership with India is of vital importance, and we are confident that it will continue to grow from strength to strength.

As we move forward into an increasingly uncertain future, India can be assured that it has no better friend and partner to meet the challenges and opportunities of today, and tomorrow, than Australia.

General Koji Yamazaki

Former Chief of Staff,
Joint Staff of the Japan Self-Defense Forces

Forging Strategic Alliances: Japan, India, and the Indo–Pacific

CURRENTLY, THE WORLD IS FACING A TURNING POINT IN history where geopolitical competitions are increasingly fiercer and various issues that require the cooperation of the whole international community have occurred. In such a world, India, which is a democracy with the largest population in the world, has realized steady economic development and holds great influence in South Asia. Additionally, India's location in the Indian Ocean gives it strategic and geopolitical importance.

I deeply understand these backgrounds, so I would like to express my respect to the leadership of India's Ministry of External Affairs and Observer Research Foundation (ORF), which have realized this dialogue, the platform integrating opinion leaders and influential words.

The Raisina Dialogue is an extremely meaningful discussion platform with the participation of ministers, senior government officers, chiefs of defence (CHODs), business executives, media personnel, and researchers and fellows from various countries; it has built the foundation of peace and stability in the region and has then contributed to global peace and stability through discussions on various issues in the Indo–Pacific region. I strongly believe that the importance of the

Dialogue will be further increased in the future.

I am pleased from the bottom of my heart that Japan and India, fulfilling such important responsibilities, share the Special Strategic and Global Partnership, and that the relationship between the two countries is being strengthened at an accelerating pace.

A UNIQUE PLATFORM

I have participated in this Dialogue four times since the fifth edition, and through the multilateral panel discussions and meetings, I had frank and open-minded discussions on the future of the global security environment with the CHODs of our allies and like-minded countries including India, which share universal values and strategic interests. This Dialogue, which provides many and various players with opportunities to meet, is extremely meaningful to deepen mutual understanding and strengthen collaboration. Especially, I remember it like it was yesterday, in the fifth edition (in 2020) I had an opportunity to meet with General Bipin Rawat, the first Chief of Defence Staff, who passed away in January of 2021 after an unfortunate accident. It was the first CHOD-level meeting for General Rawat after his appointment as the Chief of Defence Staff; however, we were able to exchange our opinions candidly. The outcomes of the meeting are reflected in our current bilateral and multilateral defence cooperation. Taking this opportunity, I would like to express my sincere respect for General Rawat.

Furthermore, I would like to stress that through meetings and discussions with CHODs, I realized that the presence of India as a geopolitical player and the expectation from the international community on the role of India has been increasing over the years.

Taking a look at the deepening of defence cooperation

between the Japan Self-Defence Force and the Indian Armed Force, under the vision of the Free and Open Indo–Pacific, Japan and India are essential to realizing a rules-based and free and open international order and securing peace and stability in the region. I recognize that India is currently seeking to establish a joint force based on the Joint Doctrine of the Indian Armed Forces in 2017. Simultaneously, the Japan Self-Defense Force is striving to strengthen its joint operation postures, represented by the establishment of the Permanent Joint Headquarters (PJHQ). Under these movements, the first Japan–India Joint Staff Talks were held in September of this year. As a former Chief of Staff, Japan Joint Staff, I am delighted from the bottom of my heart to see the start of joint-level cooperation between Japan and India—which was my earnest desire. Such developments in Japan–India cooperation will provide the Raisina Dialogue with new opportunities for dialogue and discussions.

I would like to convey my congratulations, hoping that the Dialogue continues to be an 'ideas arena' for all participants in the future.

Mohammed Soliman

Director, Strategic Technologies and Cyber Security Program at the Middle East Institute, Washington, D.C.

Old Discord and the Abraham Accords: Which Shall Prevail?

THE MIDDLE EAST FINDS ITSELF IN AN UNEXPECTED GREY area. The tragic shadow of the ongoing Israel–Gaza war, long as it is, hasn't eclipsed the Abraham Accords and the other minilateral formats in the Middle East. These United States (US)-brokered agreements and formats continue to represent solid avenues for expanded regional cooperation and economic ties.

Furthermore, minilateral formats such as the I2U2 (consisting of Israel, India, the US, and the United Arab Emirates or UAE), the India–Middle East–Europe Corridor (IMEC),[1] and the Negev Forum (comprising Israel, Egypt, Morocco, Bahrain, the US and the UAE) have demonstrated resilience throughout the present crisis, potentially mitigating the disintegration of the region during the intense Israeli military campaign and its devastating civilian toll. From the Houthi's escalating attacks[2] in the

---

[1]Soliman, Mohammed, 'India's Economic Corridor to Europe via Saudi, UAE: A Win for US, West Asia', *Al-Monitor*, 11 September 2023, https://tinyurl.com/39zed8pr. Accessed on 21 August 2024.

[2]Armstrong, Kathryn, 'Houthis Claim New Attacks on Red Sea Shipping', *BBC*, February 2024, https://tinyurl.com/de36km7a. Accessed on 21 August 2024.

Red Sea to the targeting of US assets in Iraq[3] and Jordan[4] and the renewed skirmishes between Israel and Hezbollah, a chilling message echoes across regional capitals: Iran's transregional power grab poses not only an existential threat to governments but also a critical roadblock to any ambitious dreams of Middle Eastern integration. Furthermore, the Israel–Gaza war underscores the need for a regional framework that can build both long-term security and provide a political horizon for Palestinians, mitigating the likelihood of further regional violence or regional disintegration.

CRUCIAL INTERMEDIATION

Egypt has undertaken[5] a delicate balancing act in the aftermath of the Gaza conflict. While upholding its strong security and intelligence ties with Israel, Cairo has expressed solidarity with the Palestinian people and resisted[6] Israel's attempts to expel Palestinians into the Sinai Peninsula. Echoing Egypt's historical focus on maintaining internal stability, President El-Sisi's strategy prioritizes shielding Cairo from regional conflict—an approach deeply rooted in the country's long-standing security doctrine. Despite the ongoing war in Gaza and regional escalation, Saudi Arabia

---

[3]'Drone, Explosive Attacks Target US Forces Across Iraq', *Reuters*, 10 November 2023, https://tinyurl.com/y8uweuwm. Accessed on 21 August 2024.

[4]Britzky, Haley, Natasha Bertrand, and Oren Liebermann, 'Three US Troops Killed in Drone Attack in Jordan, More than 30 Injured', *CNN*, 29 January 2024, https://tinyurl.com/4r3najve. Accessed on 21 August 2024.

[5]Amin, Shahira, 'Egypt was Mediating a Deal to End the Gaza War. Then Saleh Al-Arouri was Assassinated', *Atlantic Council*, 10 January 2024, https://tinyurl.com/4xpd3p63. Accessed on 21 August 2024.

[6]Ibid.

has indicated[7] its willingness to normalize relations with Israel. In a recent interview with the BBC, the Kingdom's ambassador to the United Kingdom acknowledged[8] 'a clear interest' in pursuing diplomatic ties with Israel. However, the path to normalization has narrowed in the wake of the Gaza war, with Saudi Arabia now insisting on a viable Palestinian political solution as a precondition. This is a position that also reflects[9] the Biden administration's post-war strategy. 'The strategy post October 7 is that we want to see normalization [between Israel and Saudi Arabia] tied to a political horizon for the Palestinians,' White House National Security Advisor Jake Sullivan said at the World Economic Forum.

The other Gulf monarchies that have signed the Abraham Accords—the UAE and Bahrain—demonstrated their commitment to maintaining ties with Israel in the face of Iran's regional ambitions. Türkiye, under President Tayyip Erdogan, has maintained[10] a more critical stance towards Israel. Erdogan has denounced Israel's military campaign in Gaza; however, Türkiye's rhetoric has not been aligned with its actions, as the country continues to allow the transport of oil shipments to Israel. Hezbollah, a major Iranian proxy and one of Israel's fiercest opponents, has walked a tightrope amidst the recent Israel–Gaza conflict. Though

---

[7]Gritten, David, 'Saudi Arabia Interested in Israel Normalisation Deal After War', *BBC*, 9 January 2024, https://tinyurl.com/bdfp64ja. Accessed on 21 August 2024.

[8]Ibid.

[9]Ravid, Barak, 'Sullivan: U.S. Post-War Strategy Links Saudi-Israel Peace Deal with Two-State Solution', *Axios*, 16 January 2024, https://tinyurl.com/y5h5t8mn. Accessed on 21 August 2024.

[10]'Turkey Talks Tough on Israel but Resists Calls to Cut Off Oil', *International Report* (podcast), 11 November 2023, https://tinyurl.com/3rbvsaaw. Accessed on 21 August 2024.

distancing[11] itself from Hamas's decision to launch the October 7 attacks on Israel, it has maintained its signature low-level skirmishes along the Lebanese–Israel border. This calibrated display of force serves to appease its domestic power base without provoking an all-out war with Israel, a scenario that could devastate Lebanon's already reeling economy.

A VICIOUS CYCLE

This cycle of conflict has not only underscored the regional implications of Iran's increasing power and influence but also demonstrated its capacity to project this influence across various domains simultaneously. This development significantly affects both regional and global dynamics. Iran's mastery in orchestrating multi-front escalations through its proxies, ranging from targeting US forces in Iraq and Jordan to disrupting global shipping in the Red Sea, has raised widespread concerns among regional capitals on their own security, economic development, and prospects for regional integration. Even before the Gaza war, Gulf states recognized the risks posed by Tehran's regional threats and have sought to contain its influence by pursuing strategic alliances and rapprochement with Israel. This strategy remains prevalent today, even in the face of the escalating humanitarian crisis in Gaza and the rising Palestinian civilian toll. The deep-seated apprehension regarding Iran's expanding influence provides a strong rationale for the Abraham Accords and minilateral forums such as I2U2[12], the Negev Forum,

---

[11]Pacchiani, Gianluca, 'In Much-Hyped Speech, Nasrallah Makes Threats but Does Not Commit to Broader War', *The Times of Israel*, 3 November 2023, https://tinyurl.com/wvzppmj7. Accessed on 21 August 2024.

[12]Soliman, Mohammed, 'The I2U2 Needs Muscle. Cairo and Riyadh Can Help', *Middle East Institute*, 22 August 2022, https://tinyurl.com/2282ud6s. Accessed on 21 August 2024.

and IMEC[13]. Meanwhile, these efforts unfold against the backdrop of widespread Arab public frustration due to the ongoing crisis in Gaza.

However, the renewed Israeli–Palestinian conflict serves as a stark reminder: lasting peace and security in the Middle East requires a sustainable solution to this historical issue—or, at least, a political horizon for the Palestinian people that can give them their deserved rights and help prevent further escalation, preserving a bare minimum level of regional stability. In demonstrating just how far it is willing to go to force the Palestinian issue to remain on the table, Hamas is challenging regional and global powers to reconsider their priorities. Minilateral formats that include Israel, such as the I2U2 and IMEC, have remained mainly cohesive because the Palestinian issue has *not* been a central topic of concern. But these two paths, one towards greater regional integration and one towards a viable solution to the Israeli–Palestinian conflict, may not be mutually exclusive. Instead, the past several years of improved Arab–Israeli cooperation under the Abraham Accords have offered a taste of the formidable security and economic benefits that result from regional integration. A desire to continue enjoying these benefits may lend necessary momentum for key actors to pursue a pathway for sustainable peace.

A PATHWAY EMERGES

These prevailing crisis points and India's growing voice in world affairs have made the Raisina Dialogue a critical pathway for conflicting parties to utilize. Not many global capitals have the diplomatic pull to host Israel, Iran, the Palestinians, and the Arab states under one roof to debate

---

[13]Ibid.

the most contentious regional and global issues. And Raisina, propelled by India's growing voice in global geopolitics, has done this consistently for nearly a decade. As we enter 2024, Raisina once again offers the opportunity to mobilize open-door debates, displaying goodwill and genuine intention for dialogue.

At this juncture, the Middle East may not choose, or perhaps even be allowed to choose, between old discord and the Abraham Accords. Instead, the region's future might lie in the nebulous terrain between the two. On the one hand, the scars of past conflicts and the enduring Palestinian question leave little room for complete trust and full regional integration. On the other hand, the burgeoning security and economic ties fostered by formats like the Abraham Accords, I2U2 and IMEC offer a glimpse of a more prosperous and stable future. The path forward will likely be one of constant negotiation, incremental progress and shrewd navigation through the volatile currents of regional power dynamics and great power competition.

Admiral John C. Aquilino

Commander, United States Indo–Pacific Command

Global Security Nexus: Unravelling Raisina's Impact

THE RAISINA DIALOGUE BRINGS TOGETHER LEADERS FROM the military, industry, politics, academia, and various other fields, and it has, over the years, emerged as an influential platform to promote multilateralism and address the most pressing security issues facing the Indo–Pacific region and beyond.

The inaugural event was held in March 2016, with Admiral Harry Harris, a predecessor and mentor of mine, serving as the keynote speaker.

Admiral Harris' keynote in 2016 was titled 'Let's Be Ambitious Together'.[1] He described actions that he believed would advance the bilateral relationship between the United States (US) and India, based on the Joint Strategic Vision signed in 2015 by Prime Minister Narendra Modi and the then US President Barack Obama. Prime Minister Modi's persistent focus on the India–US relationship and his approach to statecraft has been instrumental in maintaining the necessary momentum for not just the bilateral relationship between India and the US but also the Free and Open Indo–Pacific that he and former Prime Minister of Japan Shinzo Abe worked hard to facilitate.

---

[1]The US State Department. https://tinyurl.com/mjdkrv5z. Accessed on 14 August 2024.

Admiral Harris had then made the bold suggestion that India, Japan, Australia and the US should revive the Quadrilateral Security Dialogue, or Quad—an idea first coined by the late Prime Minister Abe in 2007. Six months later, following the discussions at the inaugural Raisina Dialogue, US Secretary of Defense Ash Carter and Indian Minister of Defence Manohar Parrikar signed the Major Defense Partner designation—a status unique to India. It institutionalized the progress made to facilitate defence trade and technology sharing to a level on par with that between the US and its closest allies and partners.

A QUADRUPLE STRATEGY

One year later, in 2017, the Raisina Dialogue hosted the first panel that included the Quad nations and an academic panellist from Indonesia. Raisina's efforts to push the boundaries on the Quad inspired Admiral Harris to recommend an official name change for the US's oldest and largest combatant command. In 2018, at Admiral Harris' change of command and retirement ceremony, Secretary of Defense Jim Mattis officially announced the name change from U.S. Pacific Command to U.S. Indo–Pacific Command, highlighting the connection and importance of the Indian and Pacific Oceans to the security landscape of the region.

Admiral Harris believed then, as I do now, that the US–India relationship represents the most significant opportunity for both countries in the twenty-first century. However, bold and audacious leadership is needed to expand and deepen the strategic partnership to harness the inherent potential of our two great democracies and the growing ties between our people, economies and governments.

Admiral Phil Davidson, my immediate predecessor, continued Admiral Harris' efforts to make Raisina a crucial incubator for multilateral conversations that senior military officers across the region must have. Six months following the Raisina Dialogue in 2018 and the announcement of the U.S. Indo–Pacific Command name change, the first-ever 'two-plus-two' meeting of the US's and India's top defence and diplomatic officials took place. The third foundational agreement, known as the Communications Compatibility and Security Agreement (COMCASA), was also signed at that time, which provides the possibility of Indian military units gaining access to a secure Common Tactical Picture, in turn allowing Indian military units to receive data from the US and friendly counterparts during exercises or operations. In January 2019, Admiral Davidson sat on the first all-military officer panel at the Raisina Dialogue, which included the Quad nations and France. The panel underscored the need for multilateral collaboration between like-minded countries to maintain stability in the security landscape and a Free and Open Indo–Pacific.

A few months later, at the second two-plus-two between India and the US, the Industrial Security Annex (ISA) was signed, allowing for the transfer of technologies supporting defence production. Additionally, the Basic Exchange and Cooperation Agreement (BECA), the latest foundational agreement that gave India expertise in geospatial intelligence, provided India the mission-planning capability to work with real-time data to defence forces when using weapons like cruise missiles, ballistic missiles and drones. Finally, Australia joined the Malabar Naval Exercise, which coincidentally sat on top of various political and military dialogues and arrangements between the Quad countries. Today, all four countries are permanent members of the Malabar Exercise, which takes place every other year at various locations in the Indian and Pacific oceans.

Following Admiral Davidson's last engagement at the

Raisina Dialogue in April 2021, he announced in his final Congressional testimony that the Indian and US navies are now securely sharing information with one another. India has substantially increased its acquisition of US defence equipment. Defence sales are at an all-time high, with India operating US-sourced platforms such as P-8A Poseidon, Precision-Guided Excalibur Munitions, and helicopters like the Apache and Chinook.

Admiral Davidson communicated to the Raisina Dialogue in 2021 that the US expects substantial progress on interoperability and information sharing, as well as service-level and joint military-to-military quadrilateral collaboration between India, Australia, Japan and the US, at a pace all four countries are willing to accept as the relationship continues to mature.

I assumed command of INDOPACOM shortly after Raisina 2021 and attended my first Raisina Dialogue in March 2022. I thoroughly enjoyed meeting with the chiefs of defence from the Quad nations, the chief of defence from the United Kingdom, and the deputy director for international affairs from France. I got to see first-hand why Raisina was so important—it provides the opportunity to meet with many allies and partners who are singularly focused on the issues facing the Indo–Pacific. Thirty days later, ORF America opened its doors in Washington, D.C., acknowledging that the US–India partnership will be a defining one for the foreseeable future, not always without its differences and difficulties, but moving together towards convergence and cooperation.

THE INDO–PACIFIC TIES

This relationship between two of the world's three largest populations, two of the world's largest militaries, and, in the near future, two of the world's largest economies will naturally have global implications. Therefore, generating a better understanding of each other's policies is imperative. This long-term investment of an 'ideas bridge' between India and the US on global issues was energized because of the Raisina Dialogue.

As the world's oldest and largest democracies, the US and India would gain from a closer partnership—one that is indispensable for promoting and maintaining global peace and prosperity. Indeed, the US–India relationship endures and continues to develop based on shared principles and a complementary vision of the future. The US views India as a critical security partner in Asia. Participants are willing to advance the US–India relationship through this dialogue based on our shared love for democracy and freedom.

A panel at this year's most recent Raisina Dialogue, titled 'The Future of Conflict: Lessons from the Third Decade', took a deeper look at the impacts of conflict on the global community on the heels of the March G20 Foreign Ministers' Meeting. Over the past two years, the United States and India have expanded their defence activities and consultations and recently concluded the last of the 'foundational defense agreements' across all the services and defence intelligence services, capping off a nearly two-decade effort by policymakers in both countries to formalize the legal sinews of operational defence cooperation.

From Harry Harris to today, the Raisina Dialogue has created the political and social space for us to witness the foreign ministers from the Quad nations discuss on a global stage the issues that concern them most. All four countries have made efforts to nurture the Quad and work towards an agenda that our governments are now working on together. Japan's foreign minister at that time, Yoshimasa Hayashi, who is a gifted pianist, referred to himself and his three colleagues as the Beatles—they all play together but can also work solo. Just 60 days after Raisina, the Quad military chiefs met again at the Indo–Pacific Security Dialogue at Sunnylands for more focused discussions on the security and political landscape and how the militaries could work closer together across the region to help build confidence, reinforce the rules-based international order, and support further regional integration.

The next Raisina Dialogue, scheduled in February 2024, will be my last as USINDOPACOM commander. I believe the relationship between the US and India has an irreversible momentum as long as the conditions continue to foster opportunities for more robust economic integration and increased military interoperability. The Raisina Dialogue will continue to play a vital part in what many believe is the most substantial bilateral relationship for the twenty-first century and a gold standard for shaping multilateral engagements, as witnessed by the Quad.

Section 5

Viral World: Outbreaks, Outliers and Out of Control

Narendra Modi

Prime Minister of India

THIS EDITION OF THE RAISINA DIALOGUE TAKES PLACE at a watershed moment in human history. A global pandemic has been ravaging the world for over a year. The last such global pandemic was a century ago. Although humanity has faced many infectious diseases since then, the world today is underprepared to handle the COVID-19 pandemic.

Our scientists, researchers and industry have answered some questions.

What is the virus?
How does it spread?
How can we slow it down?
How do we make a vaccine?
How do we administer vaccines at scale and with speed?

To these and many other such questions, many solutions have emerged. And no doubt many more are yet to come. But as global thinkers and leaders, we must ask ourselves some more questions.

For over a year now, the best minds of our societies have been engaged in battling this pandemic. All the governments of the world at all levels are trying to contain and control this pandemic. Why did it come to this? Is it perhaps because, in the race of economic development, the concern for the welfare of humanity has been left behind? Is it perhaps because, in the age of competition, the spirit of cooperation has been forgotten?

The answer to such questions can be found in our

recent past. Friends, the horrors of the First and Second World Wars compelled the emergence of a new world order. After the end of the Second World War, over the next few decades, many structures and institutions were created, but under the shadow of the two wars, they were aimed at answering only one question: how to prevent the Third World War?

Today I submit to you that this was the wrong question; as a result, all the steps taken were like treating a patient's symptoms without addressing the underlying causes. Or to put it differently, all the steps taken were to prevent the last war, not the next one. In fact, while humanity has not faced a Third World War, the threat of violence has not reduced in people's lives. With a number of proxy wars and unending terror attacks, the prospect of violence is ever-present.

So what would have been the right questions? These could have included:

Why do we have famines and hunger?
Why do we have poverty?
Or, most fundamentally, why can't we cooperate to address problems that threaten the entire humanity?

I'm sure that if our thinking had been along such lines, very different solutions would have emerged.

Friends, it is not too late even now. The mistakes and misdeeds of the past seven decades need not constrain our thinking for the future. The COVID-19 pandemic has presented us an opportunity to reshape the world order, to re-orient our thinking. We must create systems that address the problems of today and the challenges of tomorrow, and we must think of the entire humanity and not merely of those who are on our side of the borders. Humanity as a whole must be at the centre of our thinking and action.

Friends! During this pandemic, in our own humble way, with our own limited resources, we in India have tried to walk the talk. We have tried to protect our own 1.3 billion citizens from the pandemic. At the same time, we have also tried to support the pandemic response efforts of others. In our neighbourhood, we have encouraged our coordinated regional response to the crisis. Last year we shared medicines and protective equipment with over a hundred and fifty countries. We understand fully that mankind will not defeat the pandemic unless all of us, everywhere, regardless of the colour of our passports, come out of it. That is why, this year despite many constraints, we have supplied vaccine to over 80 countries. We know that the supplies have been modest. We know that the demands are huge. We know that it will be a long time before the entire humanity can be vaccinated. At the same time, we also know that hope matters. It matters as much to the citizens of the richest countries as it does to the less fortunate. And so we will continue to share our experiences, our expertise, and also our resources with the entire humanity in the fight against the pandemic.

Friends, as we gather virtually at the Raisina Dialogue this year, I call upon you to emerge as a powerful voice for a human-centric approach. As said elsewhere, while we may be used to having a plan A and a plan B, there is no planet B—we have only planet Earth. And so, we must remember that we hold this planet merely as trustees for future generations.

I will leave you with that thought and wish you very productive discussions over the next few days. Before I conclude, I wish to thank all the dignitaries who are adding their voices to these deliberations. My special thanks to Their Excellencies, the President of Rwanda and the Prime Minister of Denmark, for their valuable presence in this session of the Dialogue. I also wish to thank my friend the Prime Minister of Australia and the President of the European Council who will be joining the Dialogue later.

Last but not the least, my immense gratitude and heartiest congratulations to all the organizations. They have done fantastic work in putting together this year's Raisina Dialogue despite all kinds of challenges.

Thank you.

This speech was delivered at the inaugural address at the 6th Raisina Dialogue, 2021 (13 April 2021).

Mette Frederiksen

Prime Minister of Denmark

THANK YOU TO THE ORGANIZERS.

His Excellency Prime Minister Modi.

His Excellency President Kagame.

His Excellency Minister of External Affairs Jaishankar.

And to the Observer Research Foundation.

Thank you all for hosting this very important event. I am grateful for having the opportunity to speak to you today.

'In a gentle way, you can shake the world,' Gandhi once said.

The world has indeed been shaken the past year. Unfortunately not very gently. We live in the time of a global pandemic.

We also live in the time of another global challenge: climate change, a crisis more far-reaching than the pandemic. That is why climate-related security risks are expected to be a top priority if Denmark is elected for a seat in the UN Security Council in 2025. Investing in climate action is also a necessary investment in our security and prosperity.

I come from the land of Hans Christian Andersen. The land of fairy tales. In fairy tales, people have to go through difficult times in order to reach a happy ending. That is what happened to Denmark: 100 years ago, a small farmland in the North of Europe; now a green superpower. And today, I welcome India, and other countries, joining us on this journey.

We stand on the brink of a green industrial revolution with new clean energy sources and promising new technologies.

If we combine Danish skill and Indian scale with speed, scope and political will, we can launch a new era of just, green transformation.

That leads me to my message for you today: the green industrial revolution is not only necessary, it comes with great opportunities and can put millions of people to work. It can also be highly cost-effective. Allow me to elaborate.

Renewable energy creates three times more jobs than fossil fuels do, and Asia stands to secure the lion's share of those jobs. In Denmark, estimates show that installing one gigawatt of offshore wind secures almost 15,000 full-time jobs. Today, solar and onshore wind are the cheapest energy sources in most countries. Cheaper than coal. Cheaper than gas. On a windy day, Denmark can produce more than 100 per cent of our electricity needs from wind. So renewables are also a gateway to energy security.

The green energy revolution requires investments. There is no way around that. But the return on these investments is big. In fact, the savings will amount to eight times the cost when accounting for health and environmental factors.

Of course, as we say in Denmark, the greenest and cheapest energy is the energy you do not use. During the past 30 years, Denmark has managed to decouple economic growth from energy consumption. In fact, Danish GDP has increased by more than 50 per cent, while our energy consumption has decreased by 6 per cent. It is possible to create economic growth while lowering the use of energy.

On this green journey in Denmark, we have focused on creating strong cooperation between public and private actors. Without public-private cooperation, green transition will not happen. Right now, Denmark is powering ahead with building the world's first 'energy islands'. The energy islands are huge offshore wind farms—the largest, most expensive infrastructure project ever made in Denmark. Once completed, the energy island in the North Sea alone will have a capacity of 10 gigawatts. 10 gigawatts! That is close to ten times the capacity of the largest offshore wind farm in the world today, and it is enough to meet the electricity demand of about 10 million European households. The potential is even greater: In time, the North Sea could become the green power plant of the entire European continent, connecting a number of energy islands.

All this will generate jobs. Lots of jobs. The Danish example of decades of green economic growth is not a fairy tale. It is real. This decade, we are ending coal in our energy production. By 2050, we have decided to end oil and gas production in the North Sea. Other countries can do it too.

To use the words of Prime Minister Modi, we must 'reform, transform and perform'. Governments, individuals and businesses have to come together. We must join forces across the globe. The Green Strategic Partnership between India and Denmark is an example of how we can achieve results by working together. It is an honour that the partnership is the first ever of its kind for both our countries—and hopefully, it will not be the last. Together, we aim to shake the world gently towards a green industrial revolution. Denmark is proud to support India's visions for a greener future. One example is the International Solar Alliance.

Climate change is global. It affects us all. But we also know that it affects some more than others. The world's poorest people and countries have contributed the least to climate change, but often they are hit the hardest. Without massive and rapid action, climate change will undermine the possibility of reaching the sustainable development goals. We—the international community—must raise our ambitions to address climate change and its negative impacts, particularly in vulnerable countries. We must meet our climate finance obligations. COP26 offers an opportunity to work on this. We must all do our part.

Prime Minister Modi, dear friends, the past year has been challenging. But today, we can join the new era of opportunity. Together, we can pave the way for a greener and safer future for all of us, bringing skill, scale, scope and speed into the global green transformation.

And let me end as I began—with Gandhi's words: 'We must become the change that we want to see.'

Thank you.

This speech was delivered at the inaugural address at the 6th Raisina Dialogue, 2021 (13 April 2021).

Paul Kagame

President of Rwanda

I AM HONOURED TO ADDRESS THIS YEAR'S RAISINA Dialogue.

I thank Prime Minister Modi, the Government of India, and the Observer Research Foundation for the invitation.

I was very much looking forward to joining you physically. But the need to hold this year's event in a virtual format highlights the reality that the COVID-19 pandemic is not yet over.

Access to vaccines is highly unequal. In a situation of scarcity, power and wealth will always set the tempo.

India, despite its own challenges, has produced most of the vaccine doses sent to Africa, under COVAX and related programmes.

Without India's production capacity and spirit of solidarity, it is possible that Africa would not have received the required quantity of vaccines at all.

This unsustainable situation demonstrates the opportunity for more ambitious private-sector investments between India and Africa, in pharmaceutical manufacturing among other areas.

The relationship between India and Rwanda continues to flourish, and our goal is to further deepen our ties.

Rwanda and India continue to collaborate on important infrastructure and development initiatives.

The key objective is to increase the educational and employment opportunities available to young people in both India and Rwanda.

Knowledge, innovation, and the green economy will still be the key drivers of growth after the pandemic.

The Observer Research Foundation's annual Kigali Global Dialogue is another good example. This event brings a fresh perspective to global debates on development and growth, and attests to the increasing multipolarity of our world. I hope that many of you will attend Kigali for its next edition in 2022.

In the meantime, I wish you fruitful deliberations at this year's Raisina Dialogue.

This speech was delivered at the inaugural address at the 6th Raisina Dialogue, 2021 (13 April 2021).

Charles Michel

Former President of the European Council

INTERNATIONAL AFFAIRS AND PLAYERS ARE CHANGING, and they're making their presence felt. For instance, India often comes up in the debates of the European Council, even when it is not on the agenda. Why is that? Because in a world that's more interconnected and competitive but less stable, like-minded countries tend to look out for each other and join forces. We see, more clearly than ever, the need for global cooperation and for rules-based international order. Unfortunately, not everyone is choosing this path.

In many ways, the path of the future world order will be set in the Indo–Pacific region. This region has become a global economic and political centre of gravity, and the European Union (EU) is closely linked to it through trade, investment and mobility. We have a large stake in its freedom, openness and stability. The EU is about to set out, for the first time, a comprehensive strategic approach to this region.

As the two largest democracies in this challenging landscape, India and the European Union are key partners. We can and we should do much more together. First, to make the world a better, fairer and safer place. We value human rights, equal opportunities, gender equality and the rule of law. We share the same multilateralist DNA. The EU is the result of a patient association of sovereign countries. We are united by our will to join forces and cooperate based on commonly agreed-upon rules. And second, it is in our mutual interest to maximize the untapped potential of trade and investment between our two major economies.

Concretely, we propose to focus on four strains of cooperation: COVID-19, fighting climate change, boosting our economic cooperation, and security and peace.

In the past, the planet saw as its most pressing challenge the COVID-19 pandemic, including the production of vaccines and their delivery to all regions and countries of the world. Both India and Europe were and continue to be major producers of vaccines. Together, through COVAX, we were able support low- and middle-income countries in their vaccination efforts. Thanks to our joint efforts, more than 38 million doses of COVAX was delivered to 100 countries across the globe.

We all know that ramping up production of the vaccine was an enormous challenge, and we all needed each other for components and equipment, and to fill and finish vials, for instance. The crisis taught us why we must make sure that our supply chains remain open and resilient. This includes expanding global manufacturing capacity in the pharmaceutical sector, especially in developing countries.

In the longer term, we must be better prepared. This is why I launched the idea of an international treaty on pandemics, which would be anchored in the World Health Organization. Along with Dr Tedros Ghebreyesus, we gathered the support of 26 leaders from five continents.

ENGAGING PARTNERSHIPS

The pandemic was the first of our many problems. The world, as most of my peers agree, faces much more crucial and testing times ahead. The most ravaging topic has become the very essence of human survival in the face of a warming planet, rapid climate change, and the economic shifts we experience today.

In this quest, the EU was the first to commit to climate

neutrality by 2050. This is a pledge to our people but also to the rest of the world. The European Green Deal, along with our digital agenda, is at the heart of our economic recovery strategy. Yet, fighting climate change and stopping the loss of biodiversity require the leadership of all major economies. This is why we are striving for a joint EU–India commitment to green growth, circular economy and clean energy. This will be needed all over the world and will create jobs and economic opportunities.

We also want to be a leader in the space of digital revolution, industrial data, connected objects and artificial intelligence. But in this transition, we must avoid the mistakes of past transitions, namely abusing our digital resources like we abuse our natural resources. In this field, like in others, the EU has developed a global standard-setting capacity: the so-called Brussels effect. I propose that we work with like-minded partners on this democratic digital standard, and I see India as a key partner in this endeavour.

On the economic front, the EU is India's first trading partner and foreign investor, and we are ready to develop our huge potential for more trade, more jobs and more growth. This will make our economies more resilient.

The EU is not just an economic partner; we are also determined to play our role in the security of the Indo–Pacific region. We are engaged in securing peace in Afghanistan. We call for restoring the democratic process in Myanmar. In Iran, the EU played a key role, and we remain a strong defender of the JCPOA. Nuclear proliferation is still a major concern, including the nuclear activities of North Korea. Some 40 per cent of our trade passes through the Indian Ocean, so we have a strong interest in maritime security in the region.

Our friendship and partnership with India are a cornerstone of our geopolitical strategy. We are determined to further develop the ties between our peoples. It is in our common interest to show that the democratic and open model is the most powerful one to address the challenges of the world.

This speech was delivered as the keynote address at the 6th Raisina Dialogue, 2021 (14 April 2021).

Section 6

Unblurred Vision: Development with a Difference

Kwame Owino and Jackline Kagume

CEO, Institute of Economic Affairs (IEA)
Constitution, Law and Economy Programme Head at
IEA Kenya

African Union at the G20 High Table: Implications for the Future of Economic Governance

THE RAISINA DIALOGUE HAS PROVIDED AN INVALUABLE platform for global thought leaders to deliberate upon and propose solutions to common challenges, furthering cooperation on complex and evolving economic governance issues. For most of the Global South, this ambition is reflective of India's demonstrated commitment to advancing pluralism and advocating for the interests of the South at global multilateral forums. As exemplified by its support for the admission of the African Union (AU) into the G20 during its presidency, India has sought to amplify the voices of emerging economies and promote inclusivity in global economic governance.

In the face of increasing fragilities in the global ecosystem, India has remained resolute in its rejection of deglobalization, instead advocating for inclusion and cooperation for collective problem-solving. Most significantly, while India's profile and influence are rising globally, it has remained unapologetic about being a democracy in a moment where the global narrative is that democracy is impractical for developing countries. It has also stood against open attempts by a few nations to denigrate democratic institutions and to make African countries cynical about democracy. India has continued to give legitimacy to democracy and to promote democratic ideals as the sustainable path to development, despite the current global challenges.

Before the admission of the AU, the Group of 20 (G20) was an influential coalition of 19 sovereign countries and the European Union (EU). Since its formation in 1999, the G20 has focused on providing a forum that pursues consensus among influential economic actors to achieve better global economic governance. The rationale for this form of cross-country cooperation was emphasized in the New Delhi Leaders' Declaration[1], which was adopted on 9 September 2023 during the G20 New Delhi Summit. It stated, 'G20 cooperation is essential in determining the course that the world takes.'

For a coalition of sovereign nations and the EU, the absence of Sub-Saharan Africa was conspicuous; this was corrected by the invitation to the AU to represent the continent of Africa in the G20. The World Economic Forum acknowledged that the admission of the AU gives the continent an 'important voice on key global issues'.[2] This symbolic admission raises a pertinent question: what does AU's admission mean for the future of economic governance?

Among all continents, the African continent, in general, and the countries of Sub-Saharan Africa, in particular, are the least embedded in global economic affairs and

---

[1]'G20 New Delhi Leaders' Declaration', *G20 India*, September 2023, https://tinyurl.com/3jb6wvpu. Accessed on 15 August 2024.
[2]Munyati, Chido, 'The African Union has been Made a Permanent Member of the G20 – What Does it Mean Mean for the Continent?', *World Economic Forum*, 14 September 2023, https://tinyurl.com/yts287xm. Accessed on 12 August 2024.

commerce. This can be confirmed from their smaller share in global trade in goods and services, inadequate foreign direct investment (FDI), and limited diversity in domestic economic activities. These challenges make it clear that access to regional and global markets is an indispensable part of the path to prosperity for countries represented by the AU. On the other hand, the reality of global affairs shows that geopolitical and geoeconomic headwinds are leading towards acceptance of the rising but mistaken idea that globalization was an 'error' and that its reversal is necessary to accommodate rising powers in the quest to break 'Western and US hegemony'.

However genuine the political pressures to reverse globalization may be to accommodate emerging powers, it is evident that the collective interest of the AU would be poorly served by fragmentation and deglobalization. Pascal Lamy and Nicolas Kohler-Suzuki asserted in the *Foreign Affairs*[3] that there is good reason to be 'sceptical of the doomsayers of globalisation'. Thus, the AU's accession to permanent membership ought to be used to articulate the important point that for the world to grow sceptical of globalization just as Sub-Saharan Africa gets to the front of the queue is hypocritical and would be harmful to all countries.

The AU's voice in calling for the reinforcement of multilateralism is consistent with Paragraph 47 of the New Delhi Declaration. The Declaration acknowledges the challenges that are affecting the global order and then reiterates that 'a more inclusive and reinvigorated multilateralism aimed at implementing the 2030 Agenda is essential'.[4] This statement of inclusion must be the consistent

---

[3]Lamy, Pascal, and Nicolas Köhler-Suzuki, 'Deglobalization is Not Inevitable', *Foreign Affairs*, 9 June 2022, https://tinyurl.com/3ztpd82c. Accessed on 12 August 2024.
[4]G20 New Delhi Leaders' Declaration.

refrain of the AU in the reconstituted G20.

By strongly asserting that reinvigorated multilateral institutions and processes are the desired path for improving global economic governance, the AU intends to ensure that its membership of the G20 is not only symbolically important, but also allows it to create consensus within the G20 on what is good for the continent and for the world.

OPPORTUNITY FOR GLOBAL INSTITUTIONAL REFORM

The AU's admission to the G20 holds considerable promise for advancing global institutional reforms for accelerated development. In addition to the essential recognition as a key player in the global economic platform, the membership presents a unique opportunity for the AU to assert its influence and advocate for essential reforms within economic governance institutions for a more inclusive and equitable framework. Primarily, the institutional changes should comprise establishing trade-related reforms, which focus on rebalancing trade relationships, reforming international financial institutions towards strengthening the resilience of African economies, and rethinking strategies for digital innovation to drive economic growth, in cognizance of Africa's demographic dividend.

As previously constituted, the G20 accounted for over 85 per cent of global GDP[5] and 75 per cent of global trade. With the admission of the AU, the collective economic influence of the now G21 has amplified. The AU should explore the G20's strategic objectives[6] under economic

---

[5]Munyati, 'The African Union has been Made a Permanent Member of the G20 – What Does it Mean Mean for the Continent?'

[6]Owino, Kwame, and Jackline Kagume, 'African Union at the G20 High

policy coordination and international cooperation to drive reforms for expanded international trade. The AU should also propose reforms to the World Trade Organization (WTO), which will work towards the gradual elimination of trade barriers and securing commitments against increasingly protectionist trends. This advocacy might mean the extension of existing preferential trade agreements to cover the entire AU, leveraging initiatives such as the African Continental Free Trade Area (AfCFTA). The trade-related reforms would not only stimulate economic growth within Africa, but also contribute to a more inclusive global economic governance framework.

Many African countries currently face various fiscal challenges, including high levels of public debt, that leave limited fiscal space for critical investments in infrastructure and provision of public services. Exacerbated by weak governance structures and systemic corruption, this has not only affected economic stability but also considerably discouraged foreign investment. As a member of the G20, the AU has the opportunity to advocate for fundamental reforms within institutions like the International Monetary Fund (IMF), the World Bank, and other multilateral institutions to address the persistent economic challenges facing African countries. Through the platform, the AU may propose comprehensive debt restructuring programmes[7] and advocate for sustainable financing and open government initiatives for enhanced transparency and accountability. The AU should also advocate for flexible financing models tailored

---

Table: Implications for the Future of Economic Governance', Observer Research Foundation, https://tinyurl.com/3s48ar3h. Accessed on 10 February 2024.

[7]Georgieva, Kristalina, and Ceyla Pazarbasioglu, 'The G20 Common Framework for Debt Treatments Must be Stepped Up', *IMF*, 2 December 2021, https://tinyurl.com/5yndwrvp. Accessed on 12 August 2024.

to the current economic realities of African countries and inclusive development policies aligned with the Sustainable Development Goals (SDGs).

The inclusion of the AU in the G20 could introduce a reconsideration of strategies for digital innovation, especially considering the immense potential of Africa's youthful population to propel economic growth. With a favourable demographic landscape characterized by a substantial young population, the AU's participation in the G20 could drive a collective shift towards prioritizing and amplifying digital innovation. This strategic realignment may involve advocating for increased investments in technology infrastructure, building literacy for emerging digital technologies, and creating a conducive environment for the growth of technology-driven enterprises. The reforms should target key domestic and global institutions, including central banks for the modernization of monetary policies, financial regulatory bodies for enhanced oversight in the financial sector, and government agencies responsible for trade. In addition, international organizations such as the IMF and the World Bank could embrace digital technology reforms by using technology to build a transparent, interconnected ecosystem to better support member countries. The adoption of advanced digital technology[8] reforms could mean accelerated development of African states and other emerging economies. Through these reforms, the AU within the G20 could advocate for initiatives that not only position Africa as a key player in the global digital economy, but also contribute significantly to economic advancement.

---

[8]'70 Per Cent of Africans Make a Living Through Agriculture, and Technology Could Transform Their World', *The Rockefeller Foundation*, 6 May 2016, https://tinyurl.com/4kmpxzu7. Accessed on 12 August 2024.

Camila dos Santos

*International Relations Advisor at
Rio de Janeiro City Hall*

Gender Equality and Politics of Care: Why It Matters for G20 and the World

THE UPCOMING G20 SUMMIT IN BRAZIL WILL FOCUS ON fostering social inclusion, combating hunger and poverty, enabling a just energy transition, promoting sustainable development, and reforming multilateral institutions as general priorities. Cutting across all these agendas, it is crucial to discuss the impact of gender inequality and its effects on exacerbating the various crises currently faced.

Globally, men possess 50 per cent more wealth than women and dominate positions of political and economic power,[1] with only 18 per cent of ministers, 24 per cent of parliamentarians, and around 34 per cent of managerial positions worldwide being occupied by women. These figures reveal an entrenched inequality perpetuated by the uneven distribution of unpaid domestic and caregiving work.[2] According to Oxfam (2020), women and girls—especially those living in poverty and belonging to marginalized groups—dedicate 12.5 billion hours daily to unpaid caregiving work, along with many additional hours of work in exchange

---

[1]Coffey, Clare, et al., 'Time to Care: Unpaid and Underpaid Care Work and the Global Inequality Crisis', *Oxfam International*, 2020, https://tinyurl.com/u27xvtn5. Accessed on 12 August 2024.
[2]Ibid.

for inadequate and unequal wages. The caregiving work performed by these women not only sustains families and ensures a healthy and productive workforce for society, but also contributes at least US$10.8 trillion to the global economy.[3]

Given the immense productive power of the care economy, one of the key points for discussions at this year's G20 will be combating gender inequality and understanding that this issue is at the heart of the fight against poverty and the promotion of truly sustainable development.

Historically, the social organization of care work has proven to be unjust and unequal, as women are often assigned the primary or exclusive responsibility for these activities. Black women and female immigrants bear an even heavier burden of physical strain, as Françoise Vergés alerts us to the feminization and racialization of the cleaning industry worldwide. When asking 'Who cleans the world?', Vergés reminds us that cleaning and caregiving practices have become inseparable from an economy that divides bodies between those entitled to good health and those whose health does not matter.[4]

Limited opportunities reflect the disproportionate caregiving responsibilities attributed to girls and women, hindering their education and employment. Time devoted to caregiving creates barriers, perpetuating multidimensional poverty and inequalities in gender, class, race, ethnicity and territory. In Brazil, women invest nearly 22 hours weekly in unpaid domestic and caregiving tasks, compared to men's 11 hours.[5] Black women, in particular, allocate even more

---

[3]Ibid.

[4]Vergès, Françoise, 'Un féminisme décolonial', *La Fabrique Éditions*, 2019.

[5]'Governo lança grupo para elaborar a Política Nacional de Cuidados', *Gov.br*, 23 May 2023, https://tinyurl.com/mrymwz47. Accessed on 12 August 2024.

time, totalling 23.5 hours each week, as per the Brazilian Institute of Geography and Statistics (IBGE) data.

In the rest of the world, the outlook does not appear more promising. According to the Global Gender Gap Report 2023, at the current pace of progress, it will take 131 years to achieve full gender equality worldwide. The World Economic Forum itself recommends increasing women's economic participation and achieving gender equality in leadership positions[6] as key factors to address broader gender gaps in families, societies and economies.

To reverse this unequal situation, governments will need to expand and improve public policies, such as providing access to affordable childcare, parental leave, and healthcare and eldercare services, aiming to promote the well-being of individuals and the economy as a whole. Additionally, various actions must be promoted, including ensuring decent work for all caregivers,[7] recognizing and redistributing unpaid domestic and caregiving work, expanding incentives for increased education and school attendance, ensuring the qualification and retention of girls and women in competitive jobs, and upholding the right to family planning and reproductive health.

However, the immense challenge of addressing care economy issues in G20 decision-making reveals that gender inequalities also manifest differently on a geographic scale. While Europe (76.3 per cent) and North America (75 per cent) lead in gender parity globally, the Middle East and North Africa (62.6 per cent) are the most unequal

---

[6]World Economic Forum, *Global Gender Gap Report 2023*, June 2023, https://tinyurl.com/459zcpn7. Accessed on 12 August 2024.

[7]Addati, Laura, et al., 'Care Work and Care Jobs for the Future of Decent Work', *ILO*, June 2018, https://tinyurl.com/yyfeeeuv. Accessed on 12 August 2024.

regions for women to live in as of 2023.[8] This indicates that efforts towards gender equity should also guide the long-awaited reform of the multilateral system, another central theme on the G20 agenda this year. The historical under-representation of women in high-level positions in multilateral organizations—especially those from the Global South—significantly impacts how solutions are presented, negotiated and implemented in their respective territories. After all, if women are the primary caretakers and contributors to the survival of our societies, they should also have a say in how those societies are governed.

Regarding this matter, the Blue Smoke initiative sheds light on elections and appointments to high-level positions within the United Nations (UN) and emphasizes that, as of 2022, the representation of women in the UN system was 46.6 per cent. However, this did not signify a step towards equity. While there are organizations within the UN system that have never been led by a woman,[9] the effort to ensure women are represented in all aspects of leadership and decision-making is an even more critical priority. When examining the four main UN bodies coordinating global action on climate change, development and biodiversity— the United Nations Development Programme (UNDP), the United Nations Environment Programme (UNEP), the Food and Agriculture Organization of the United Nations (FAO), and the Convention on Biological Diversity (CBD)—Blue Smoke found that, collectively, these four bodies had only 20 per cent female appointments in high-level positions.[10]

---

[8]World Economic Forum, *Global Gender Gap Report 2023*.

[9]Medeiros, Júlia Hara, and Nayifa Nihad, 'Unveiling Inequalities: A Spotlight on Senior Appointments at Key UN Environment and Development Bodies', *Blue Smoke*, 2023, https://tinyurl.com/3xbbfr6z. Accessed on 12 August 2024.

[10]Ibid.

By recognizing care as an essential public good crucial to the economy of our societies and states, world leaders will have the opportunity to place the guarantee of the right to care and exist at the core of their strategies. This approach will be crucial not only in the pursuit of gender equality but also in sustaining our populations in current and future challenges, such as the path towards a fair and inclusive climate transition.[11] The impact of global climate and health emergencies, coupled with the caregiving challenges of a progressively ageing population and the implementation of state austerity measures that reduce public investment in social security, has intensified the crisis for individuals in caregiving roles. Thus, the assurance of care to the workforce is an increasingly pressing issue of public policy.

In 2023, under the G20's Indian presidency, the embrace of 'women-led development' highlighted the pivotal role played by women entrepreneurs in propelling national economies.[12] The concept recognizes the crucial contributions of women to GDP growth, job creation and the provision of essential goods and services. As Brazil assumes control of the G20 presidency this year, leveraging this approach to include the politics of care is a must.

In this context, the forthcoming edition of the Raisina Dialogue, organized by the ORF in collaboration with the Ministry of External Affairs (MEA), assumes the crucial mission of serving as a strategic platform to fortify India's leadership in the global paradigm shift towards women-led development.

---

[11]Turquet, Laura, et al., 'Feminist Climate Justice: A Framework for Action', *UN Women*, 2023, https://tinyurl.com/yjazah6n. Accessed on 12 August 2024.

[12]Ravi, Shamika, and Arundhatie Biswas Kundal, eds., 'The ORF Gender Compendium: India's G20 Presidency and Women-Led Development', *Observer Research Foundation*, September 2023, https://tinyurl.com/ywzk23x7. Accessed on 12 August 2024.

Achieving this objective goes beyond being advisable; it demands a fundamental reassessment of our multilateral framework. This entails not just rethinking our approach from a decolonized and gender equality perspective but also actively integrating more female experts and practitioners from the Global South into the discussion and decision-making table, which the Raisina Dialogue has taken strides to achieve over the course of the 10 years of its existence.

It's essential to recognize that care is both a need and a right for all human beings. Our ability to navigate through present and upcoming crises depends on acknowledging that the responsibility for care work is not—and cannot be—restricted by gender. In 2024, the G20 will make strides towards reducing inequalities if it can acknowledge and take action to ensure care is recognized as a public good and a responsibility of states, essential to the economy and the preservation of life in our societies. Overcoming gender inequalities requires enabling women to have the freedom and enjoyment of their time and rights in other aspects of life. It is a right for all women, besides being economically necessary for our survival in society.

THE CHALLENGE OF THE G20'S BRAZILIAN PRESIDENCY

Leading the G20 in 2024, Brazil presides over the debut of the Women's Empowerment Working Group[13] on the Sherpa Track. The initiative, first presented during the Indian presidency, has generated expectations for broad international cooperation on the topic. Among the group's priorities are equality, economic autonomy for women,

---

[13]'Framework and Women's Empowerment: WG Proposals Well Received', *G20 Brasil*, https://tinyurl.com/4nrffnxt. Accessed on 12 August 2024.

combating misogyny and violence, and climate justice.

At the federal level, the Brazilian government has also been leading an initial but promising effort to redesign its care policy. In addition to consultations and a call for public participation, the Brazilian government has established an inter-ministerial working group to define the components that will structure and organize the National Care Policy in Brazil.[14] The Care Working Group (GTI-Cuidados) is composed of 15 federal government agencies and three research entities, which, by the end of 2024, are expected to assess the current availability of care and the urgent needs of Brazilian women.

Both initiatives could position Brazil as a necessary leader in this issue, especially among the countries of the Global South, but this does not diminish the challenges to be faced. After all, the G20 is a group led by consensus, and it will be crucial for the member countries to agree on how to deliver and advance more equitable policies for women. This effort must be seen as an intersectoral construction, to be shaped by both governments and civil society.

In this regard, the recommendations arising from the G20 engagement groups will be crucial. Beyond the efforts of Women 20, these groups, such as Business 20, Think 20 and Civil 20, have already incorporated gender equality as a cross-cutting action in their discussions. This underscores the importance of an inclusive approach involving various sectors for meaningful progress.

---

[14]'Governo lança grupo para elaborar a Política Nacional de Cuidados', *Gov.br*, 23 May 2023, https://tinyurl.com/mrymwz47. Accessed on 12 August 2024.

Nitya Mohan Khemka

Director, Program for Appropriate Technology in Health (PATH), and Lecturer, University of Cambridge

Why Women Must Lead Development Banks

IN THE EVOLVING LANDSCAPE OF GLOBAL FINANCE, development banks play a pivotal role in shaping economic and social policies. They are important in fostering economic development, reducing poverty, and addressing socio-economic challenges by facilitating investment in key sectors, supporting infrastructure development and promoting sustainable practices in the regions they serve. Despite the critical importance of these institutions, women are significantly under-represented in their leadership. This commentary argues for the necessity of women leading development banks, not merely for the sake of gender equality but for the strategic, diverse perspectives they bring, which are essential for inclusive and effective development strategies.

Historically, the banking and financial sectors have been male-dominated fields. A recent BCG study[1] found that women are significantly under-represented in senior finance functions. This gender disparity extends to leadership roles in development banks. According to a report by the Official

---

[1] Oberauer, Anna, Juliet Grabowski, and Alexander Roos, 'Finance Functions Need More Women Leaders. Here's Why', *BCG*, 17 November 2022, https://tinyurl.com/mufffemp. Accessed on 13 August 2024.

Monetary and Financial Institutions Forum[2], only 14 per cent of top positions in global financial institutions are held by women. This under-representation is not reflective of a lack of capability, but rather systemic and structural barriers and biases that have long excluded women from these roles, including negative stereotypes, limited opportunities for mentorship, a lack of support networks to facilitate career progression, work-life-balance challenges, and a lack of representation in the top financial sector jobs. Addressing the under-representation of women in senior financial positions requires a concerted effort from both financial institutions and the wider society to challenge biases, create supportive environments, and actively promote gender diversity and inclusion.[3]

BENEFITS OF WOMEN IN LEADERSHIP ROLES

Diverse leadership in financial institutions correlates with better performance and innovation. The benefits[4] of having women in leadership positions are well-known—they bring a diversity of perspectives, enhanced creativity and decision-making, greater resilience, better employee engagement and morale, a broader market understanding, and improved financial performance. A McKinsey & Company report[5]

---

[2]Horwood, Clive, 'Only 14% of Financial Institutions Headed by Women', *OMFIF*, 29 April 2022, https://tinyurl.com/34ry5e3c. Accessed on 13 August 2024.

[3]Whiting, Kate, 'This is How Inclusion Benefits the Global Economy, According to Experts at Davos', *World Economic Forum*, 30 January 2024, https://tinyurl.com/53k82wks. Accessed on 13 August 2024.

[4]Grabowski, Oberauer, and Roos, 'Finance Functions Need More Women Leaders. Here's Why'.

[5]Hunt, Dame Vivien, et al., 'Delivering Through Diversity', McKinsey & Company, 18 January 2018, https://tinyurl.com/4zxmm2rr. Accessed on 13 August 2024.

highlighted that companies with more diverse executive teams are 33 per cent more likely to see better-than-average profits. Women in leadership roles serve as role models[6] and inspire other women to pursue leadership positions. Their presence can encourage young women to aspire to leadership roles and break through barriers. For instance, the current first deputy managing director of the International Monetary Fund (IMF) Gita Gopinath's tenure at the IMF[7] exemplifies the positive impact of female leadership in a global financial institution.

However, gender balance within the development bank sector (as well as all other financial sectors) is a long way off and is damaging institutions.

Women bring different life experiences and perspectives, which can lead to more holistic and inclusive decision-making.

Women leaders often emphasize empathy and emotional intelligence, which are crucial for understanding and addressing the multifaceted challenges faced by developing nations. Their approach to risk management can be more cautious and thorough, leading to more sustainable long-term strategies. A study by the IMF[8] indicated that the presence of women in leadership roles in financial institutions contributes to the financial stability and governance of the institutions.

Research has shown that women are better able to deal with difficult relationships and situations and are more likely

---

[6]Dasgupta, Nilanjana, and Shaki Asgari, 'Seeing is Believing: Exposure to Counterstereotypic Women Leaders and its Effect on the Malleability of Automatic Gender Stereotyping', *Journal of Experimental Social Psychology* Vol. 40, No. 5, 2004, pp. 642–58.

[7]Ratna Sahay et al., 'Banking on Women Leaders: A Case for More?', *IMF Working Papers*, No. 199, 2017, https://tinyurl.com/yhedsjns. Accessed 13 August 2024.

[8]Profeta, Paola, 'Gender Equality in Decision-Making Positions: The Efficiency Gains', *Intereconomics*, Vol. 52, No. 1, 2017, pp. 34–37, https://tinyurl.com/4xe7u333. Accessed 13 August 2024.

to pay close attention to others' needs—skills necessary for respectful and constructive relationships between development banks and their beneficiaries. The same study also showed women are inclined towards the prevention and resolution of conflicts, more readily share views with others, and make efforts to reach agreement. These are all necessary components of a successful partnership and are particularly important in the development sector, which often sees banks working with vulnerable or disadvantaged people who may be left open to exploitation.

ECONOMIC AND SOCIAL IMPACTS

Empirical evidence suggests that women-led banks can significantly influence development outcomes. These institutions often focus more on social development and gender equality, which are key drivers of overall economic growth. For example, under the leadership of women, development banks have been more inclined to invest in women-centric economic initiatives, thereby empowering a significant but often neglected demographic.

Female-run small- and medium-sized enterprises (SMEs) have enormous potential in underdeveloped and developing nations. In Africa alone, they account for 60 per cent of the continent's entire GDP,[9] as well as represent most jobs held by its nationals. This impressive figure is despite a serious lack of funding. Barely 20 per cent of African women SME founders have access to any formal form of investment, which amounts to a US$42 billion financing gap. The African Development Bank Group is just one

---

[9]African Banker, 'Releasing the Huge Potential of Female-Run SMEs', *African Business*, 10 August 2023, https://tinyurl.com/ytvx75r7. Accessed on 15 August 2024.

development bank seeking to address this through their Affirmative Finance Action for Women in Africa (AFAWA) scheme, and their newly appointed Director of the Gender, Women and Civil Society Department, Malado Kaba,[10] has over 25 years of experience in international development and finance, covering public policy, macroeconomic policies, and gender and development strategies.

Several women have broken through these barriers and led development banks effectively. For instance, Ngozi Okonjo-Iweala's leadership at the World Bank brought significant changes in its approach to development financing,[11] focusing more on sustainable and inclusive growth. Her impact highlights the positive changes that can occur under female leadership.

Kristalina Georgieva[12] served as the CEO of the World Bank from 2017 to 2019, before leaving to become the managing director of the IMF—the first figure from an emerging economy to do so. Throughout her career, Georgieva has focused on the climate crisis and its link to financial stability and rising debt levels in Africa; she is now an important figure for socially responsible development and funding.

Odile Renaud-Basso[13] became the president of the

---

[10]'The African Development Bank Appoints Ms Malado Kaba Director of the Gender, Women and Civil Society Department', *African Development Bank Group*, 20 May 2022, https://tinyurl.com/bfhn9cb5. Accessed on 15 August 2024.

[11] *World Bank*, https://www.worldbank.org/en/news/press-release/2010/12/15/world-banksfund-for-the-poorest-receives-almost-50-billion-in-record-funding

[12]'Kristalina Georgieva is the sole contender to be the IMF's next boss', *The Economist*, 12 September 2019, https://tinyurl.com/2ht3wwhm. Accessed on 21 August 2024.

[13]'EBRD President Odile Renaud-Basso', *European Bank for Reconstruction and Development*, https://tinyurl.com/bdvkksrc. Accessed on 21 August 2024.

European Bank for Reconstruction and Development (EBRD) in November 2020, marking a significant milestone as the first female president of the bank. Her own areas of expertise include accelerating climate change mitigation and adaptation and leveraging economic and financial systems for sustainability.

As shown by the careers of each of these formidable women, female leaders within the development sector often prioritize sustainable and equitable development, focusing on long-term solutions that benefit both present and future generations.

STRATEGIES FOR PROMOTING WOMEN IN LEADERSHIP

Despite the clear benefits, women face numerous obstacles in reaching leadership positions in development banks. While the gender pay gap is a long-standing issue, the focus is on nuanced solutions beyond equal pay for equal work. This involves addressing the 'motherhood penalty', ensuring transparency in pay structures, and dismantling systemic barriers that women face in higher-paying industries and roles. Addressing these systemic barriers is crucial for enabling more women to ascend to these influential roles.

To increase female representation in leadership roles, development banks and governments must implement targeted strategies. These could include mentorship, sponsorship and networking programmes, policies promoting work-life balance, and initiatives to address unconscious bias in hiring and promotion processes. It is also important to support education and skill development initiatives for women, including access to higher education, training programmes, and professional development opportunities in fields relevant to STEM (science, technology, engineering and math) training and development leadership.

Female role models should also be showcased to inspire other women to pursue leadership positions.

The Raisina Dialogue is uniquely positioned to address the question of gender parity. By providing a platform to diverse voices from around the globe, Raisina allows for nuanced discourse on strategies to dismantle the systematic barriers women face in entering senior finance roles. Being multi-stakeholder and cross-sectoral in nature, the Dialogue provides a platform for high-level advocacy, where the case can be effectively put forward that the issue of under-representation is not just a question of equality; it is also a matter of existential import for development banks, which need women in senior ranks to remain relevant, effective and efficient in the twenty-first century.

The need for women to lead development banks is also a matter of efficiency and effectiveness in development financing. Women bring unique and valuable perspectives that can drive more inclusive and sustainable development strategies. It is imperative for the global community to recognize and act on this necessity by breaking down barriers and creating pathways for women to ascend to critical leadership roles.

Section 7

At the Helm of Power: India, Raisina
and the New Way Forward

Tanja Fajon

Deputy Prime Minister of Slovenia

Stepping outside the Bubble: India as an Ideas Arena

I HAD THE PRIVILEGE TO PARTICIPATE IN THE 2023 EDITION of the Raisina Dialogue, and I truly enjoyed the dynamic and diverse panels and side events, which provided a valuable platform to discuss the most pressing contemporary challenges. Such opportunities are extremely important since they bring together leaders and public figures from many different spheres—from politics and economics to science and civil society. To really have meaningful and innovative discussions, it is imperative to step outside our narrow professional bubbles, to look for fresh ideas, solutions and expertise, to get new experiences, and to put our own thinking into a different perspective.

I had visited India privately several times before participating in the Raisina Dialogue. My official visit simply confirmed my private experience—India welcomes its guests with open arms, embraces them with its warmth, and enriches them with the exchange of views at every level, be it in a conversation with a taxi driver on the crowded streets of Indian cities or with the ministers, academics and businesspeople at a renowned international conference.

At the 2023 Raisina Dialogue, our discussions were held under the title 'Provocation, Uncertainty, Turbulence: Lighthouse in the Tempest?', one that, much to my regret, most accurately reflects the current state of affairs in the international community. I believe that we all share a feeling of anxiety and insecurity, a feeling that so many things are getting out of control and that the world as we used to know it is somehow crumbling all around us.

The foundations of the international order, based on the United Nations (UN) Charter and international law, are shaking. The world today is increasingly complex and full of unprecedented challenges. The issues of peace and security, development, climate change and global warming, food and energy security, and pandemics are affecting us all throughout the world. There is no place in the world where one can hide and wait for these storms to pass.

Most of the challenges we are facing today or will likely face tomorrow are clearly human-made. And here lies our common responsibility and duty towards future generations. We absolutely must approach these challenges with a positive mindset or at least cope with them to the best of our abilities. We must all contribute globally, meaningfully, and in the spirit of cooperation.

Against this backdrop, I was pleased to participate in two debates that focused on the role of the UN and the importance of effective multilateralism. Slovenia is a staunch advocate of effective multilateralism with the UN at its core, and remains committed to the promotion of peace, dialogue, stability and prosperity. Our future depends on international cooperation, mutual trust and respect for norms set out in the UN Charter and international law.

To be sure, there is a strong need for more effective multilateral governance, including in terms of how the UN works. The UN system needs to become fit for the current challenges and, as such, requires reforms to perform better and more efficiently and transparently. This is something we must tackle together.

OF SINCERE PRACTICES

Like the Bled Strategic Forum (BSF)[1] that Slovenia hosts annually, the Raisina Dialogue offers interactions and exchanges with leaders, thinkers and opinion-makers from around the world. These exchanges are indispensable in addressing and finding solutions to challenges across the board.

For example, science, technology and innovation have a pivotal role in achieving progress for our societies and humanity at large. They are key to pushing forward the 2030 Agenda. The transition to a green, low-carbon economy is inconceivable without new technologies, as is an effective fight against climate change. Political goals and commitments will not be enough; it is imperative we support and embrace advances in science.

I was also delighted to participate in the Raisina Young Fellows debate regarding the type of leadership that is needed in times of instability and polarization. In my view, the leadership that we all need—nationally and internationally—should respect mutually agreed rules and norms. It should be humble, show solidarity, and promote equal opportunities. It should embrace the future in terms of technology and youth. Above all, it should always have the political will to achieve progress.

Including young people in our deliberations and decision-making processes is of vital importance. The young are our future; their numbers are growing, and so are their needs

---

[1]The Bled Strategic Forum is an intragovernmental project of the Republic of Slovenia and offers a global platform for generating ideas and exchanging views on contemporary society and its future. The conference takes place annually in the picturesque Alpine setting of Bled and is the leading forum in Central and Southeastern Europe, hosting a diverse array of regional and global stakeholders.

in terms of health, education, security and, above all, the perspective of a life of prosperity and dignity.

We should also never ignore the young generation's ideas, no matter how futuristic they sound. We should not ignore the huge political and societal potential the young have. They are powerful enough to change national political processes or bring issues to the top of the international agenda. Climate change is a prime example of this.

In the same context of inclusiveness and equality, it was important to see many influential female leaders included in the Raisina Dialogue debates. It is sad that we must point out again and again that girls and women, who make up half of the global population, need to have their rights respected and their equality promoted. Half of the global population still needs to be empowered. We need to unleash the immense potential of women and ensure their equal participation at all levels in economics, society, science and politics.

India has been at the forefront of international efforts to address and search for solutions to the problems of today's world. Its endeavours to build a bridge between the needs of developing countries and those of the developed ones during its G20 presidency have been well-noted and welcomed by Slovenia. They have also been prominently reflected in the Raisina Dialogue debates.

The slogan of India's G20 presidency, 'One Earth. One Family. One Future', corresponds well with the slogan that Slovenia chose for its campaign for non-permanent membership in the UN Security Council (2024–25), i.e. 'Building Trust. Securing Future'.

As a country with genuine interest in world affairs and with a commitment to be a reliable partner, a fair player and an honest broker, Slovenia will continue to have a constructive and close dialogue with India. We have a rich bilateral agenda and a regular high-level political dialogue, and we pursue many new avenues in business, science, technology and global cooperation.

The fact that both countries share the values of democracy, human rights, respect for international law, and effective multilateralism, and strive for a world that is secure, peaceful and prosperous, fills me with optimism.

I am pleased that the Raisina Dialogue has contributed another valuable piece to the mosaic of our bilateral relations: the partnership between the Observer Research Foundation (ORF) and the Bled Strategic Forum (BSF). India's External Affairs Minister S. Jaishankar was among the key guests at the BSF in 2021 and since then, the partnership between ORF and BSF has been a highly valued part of our bilateral cooperation. Both institutions actively participate in organizing a joint panel (one in New Delhi and one in Bled), exchanging moderators and working together to attract prominent, interesting and relevant panellists. Moreover, they provide an opportunity for young leaders to participate in deliberations.

There are so many challenges in today's world that demand credible answers and quick reactions. That is why forums such as the Raisina Dialogue are so important; they encourage frank, constructive and expert debate. Only such an exchange of views can bring us to think 'outside the box', venture down unknown roads, and find innovative solutions.

Anirban Sarma

Deputy Director, Observer Research Foundation

From the South, for the World: India's Digital Public Infrastructure

A LITTLE OVER A YEAR AGO, AT THE OUTSET OF ITS G20 presidency, India announced that promoting digital public infrastructure (DPI) would be a priority of its tenure. In particular, India was keen to advocate for a human-centric approach to technology, and to encourage greater knowledge-sharing in interlinked areas such as 'DPI, financial inclusion, and tech-enabled development'.[1] This was consonant with its efforts to champion the cause of the Global South, and to act as a unifying force for the developing world.

As the leader of the G20 in 2023, India raised an extraordinary level of global awareness about DPI through the interventions of the G20 Digital Economy Working Group, a new high-level task force on DPI,[2] and several G20 Engagement Groups. Today, the DPI model has emerged as a key Indian value proposition and is being considered, adopted or adapted by nations at very different stages of development. It is recognized as a tech innovation born in the South, whose transformative power could impact the world.

---

[1] 'G20 and India's Presidency', *Ministry of External Affairs*, 9 December 2022, https://tinyurl.com/5n65pzxc. Accessed on 10 February 2024.
[2] Sharma, Harikishan, 'Govt sets up India's G20 task force on digital public infrastructure', *The Indian Express*, 24 January 2023, https://tinyurl.com/52e4cjz2. Accessed on 14 August 2024.

TRANSFORMING INDIA

As foundational population-scale tech systems, DPIs enable the flow of individuals (through digital identity systems), money (through real-time swift payment systems), and information (through consent-based privacy-protecting data-sharing systems).[3] The pioneering architecture of India Stack helped India become the first nation to develop all three foundational DPIs—the Aadhaar unique identity, the Unified Payments Interface (UPI), and the Data Empowerment and Protection Architecture (DEPA).

Taken together, these three layers have revolutionized public service delivery, and democratized innovation on a scale never seen before. Today, Aadhaar is used by over 99.9 per cent of Indian adults to utilize public services,[4] Indians use the UPI to make 30 million transactions every day,[5] and the DEPA is changing the national credit landscape.[6] Importantly, DPIs are also driving public and private innovation by allowing the government and businesses to design new applications atop the DPI layers, and the open principles embedded in DPIs are helping create open networks in the domains of health, credit and commerce.[7]

[3]Saran, Samir, and Sharad Sharma, 'Digital Public Infrastructure: Lessons from India', *Observer Research Foundation*, 7 February 2023, https://tinyurl.com/yn228usn. Accessed on 14 August 2024.

[4]Sharma, Aman, '99.9% adults in India have Aadhaar number and "use it at least once a month", says UIDAI', *Firstpost*, 23 July 2022, https://tinyurl.com/y2dszkmr. Accessed on 14 August 2024.

[5]Yadav, Pihu, 'One billion UPI transactions per day is the near-term goal: NPCI chief', *CNBC TV18*, 29 March 2023, https://tinyurl.com/yyabuhzc. Accessed on 14 August 2024.

[6]Dixit, Siddharth, 'India's digital transformation could be a game-changer for economic development', *World Bank*, 20 June 2023, https://tinyurl.com/ydfj39k2. Accessed on 14 August 2024.

[7]Saran, Samir, and Sharad Sharma, 'Digital Public Infrastructure: Lessons from India'.

GOING GLOBAL

Given their low cost and inherent scalability, there is much interest among other nations to explore the establishment of DPIs. Platforms like the G20 have allowed India to leverage this burgeoning interest and shape it into concrete outcomes, or, at the very least, into diplomatic declarations that acknowledge DPIs' potential.

The value of DPI as an accelerator of development outcomes has been amply demonstrated.[8] India set up the Modular Open Source Identity Platform (MOSIP) in 2018 to support countries seeking to build foundational digital identity systems.[9] Today, 11 developing countries have adopted MOSIP, are drawing on Indian know-how to build their national ID platforms, and have directly benefited over 95 million citizens worldwide in the process.[10] As the G20 president, India also entered into MoUs with eight developing countries, under which it is offering them access to the India Stack architecture at no cost.[11]

It is clear, though, that the relevance of DPI transcends the Global South. In May 2023, for instance, the EU–India Trade and Technology Council acknowledged 'the importance of DPI for […] open and inclusive digital economies', and the two parties have agreed to collaborate on improving the interoperability of their respective DPIs.[12] Released in the

---

[8]'Accelerating the SDGs through Digital Public Infrastructure', *UNDP*, 21 August 2023, https://tinyurl.com/5n7eb2jv. Accessed on 14 August 2024.

[9]*MOSIP*, https://tinyurl.com/23aj6cwn. Accessed on 14 August 2024.

[10]'Country partners', *MOSIP*, https://tinyurl.com/5n83b73m. Accessed on 14 August 2024.

[11]'India enters MoUs with 8 countries to offer them Digital Stack, DPI at no cost', *The Hindu Business Line*, 5 September 2023, https://tinyurl.com/2tmsdz9u. Accessed on 14 August 2024.

[12]'India-EU Joint Statement: 1st Meeting of the Trade and Technology Council', *Ministry of External Affairs*, 16 May 2023, https://tinyurl.com/

same month, the Quad Leaders' Statement drew attention to the promise DPI held for 'sustainable development in the Indo–Pacific'.[13] The Shanghai Cooperation Organization (SCO) too has supported India's proposal to help SCO member states assess and adopt India Stack.[14]

The progress of DPI-focused bilateral engagements with advanced nations has been impressive by any standard. Following Prime Minister Modi's state visit to the United States last June, both countries announced that they intended to work together to 'provide global leadership for the implementation of DPI'.[15] Similarly, the meeting of the Indian and Japanese foreign ministers incorporated a focus on DPIs into tech partnerships that seek to build a strong and open Indo–Pacific.[16] And PM Modi's visit to France in July last year saw the two countries enter into an agreement to make the UPI fast payment switch available in France, with the objective of enabling seamless cross-border transactions, and lowering the cost of fund transfers.[17] This move made France the latest in a series of nations with whom India has UPI-related agreements, the others including Singapore, Australia, the US, the United Kingdom, Canada,

---

m2m7k6sv. Accessed on 14 August 2024.

[13]'Quad Leaders' Joint Statement', *Ministry of External Affairs*, 20 May 2023, https://tinyurl.com/bddez6mz. Accessed on 14 Augsut 2024.

[14]'SCO members adopt India's proposal for digital public infra', *Financial Express*, 14 May 2023, https://tinyurl.com/3wkkfp4x. Accessed on 14 August 2024.

[15]'Joint Statement from the United States and India', *The White House*, 22 June 2023, https://tinyurl.com/2575h7bv. Accessed on 14 August 2024.

[16]'15th India-Japan Foreign Ministers' Strategic Dialogue', *Ministry of External Affairs*, 27 July 2023, https://tinyurl.com/2n64w4z2. Accessed on 14 August 2024.

[17]'Agreement reached for using India's UPI in France: PM Modi', *Business Line*, 14 July 2023, https://tinyurl.com/ymzmh2ya. Accessed on 14 August 2024.

Hong Kong, Oman, Qatar, the United Arab Emirates, Saudi Arabia, Nepal and Bhutan.[18]

Even the United Nations[19] and other multilateral institutions like the International Monetary Fund (IMF) and the World Bank have unequivocally endorsed the DPI approach. The IMF has commended DPIs for enabling direct benefit transfers and supporting 87 per cent of India's poor households during the COVID-19 pandemic,[20] while a World Bank report concluded that India's digital infrastructure helped it achieve 80 per cent financial inclusion between 2018 and 2023—a feat that may have taken 50 years otherwise.[21]

ONWARD AND UPWARD

Speaking at the Raisina Dialogue 2023, Amitabh Kant, India's G20 Sherpa, had outlined the remarkable journey of DPI, calling it 'the model for the future' and 'an innovation from an emerging market that has overtaken the developed part of the world'.[22] Deep dives into digital breakthroughs have long been among the Raisina Dialogue's priority areas, and recent years have seen it become a pivotal platform for

---

[18]Das, Basudha, 'France adopts UPI: A look at other countries accepting UPI for cross-border transactions', *Business Today*, 15 July 2023, https://tinyurl.com/58hhx273. Accessed on 14 August 2024.

[19]'Accelerating the SDGs through Digital Public Infrastructure', UNDP.

[20]Alonso, Cristiano, et al., 'Stacking up the Benefits: Lessons from India's Digital Journey', *IMF*, 31 March 2023, https://tinyurl.com/3j8x8jmw. Accessed on 14 August 2024.

[21]'World Bank lauds India's digital public infrastructure in G20 document', *The Economic Times*, 8 September 2023, https://tinyurl.com/438ufkpn. Accessed on 14 August 2024.

[22]Kant, Amitabh, 'The Android dream: A collective approach to building digital public infrastructure', *Raisina Dialogue*, 2023, https://tinyurl.com/h2z98x6e. Accessed on 14 August 2024.

sharing international views and experiences related to DPI. It was at Raisina that some of the earliest public conversations around digital public goods and India Stack took place, and the conference continues to act as a living warehouse of ideas about technological progress and opportunities for cooperation.

With international groupings and individual nations eager to maintain the momentum generated by the Indian presidency, the next few years will see a further consolidation of global efforts to build DPIs. Building on the agreements forged in 2023, India, the European Union and the US will very likely ramp up cooperation around DPIs with a focus on strengthening capacities in third countries. Indeed, this kind of collaborative work is a much-anticipated element of the US–India Global Digital Development Partnership.[23]

The high-level 'G20 Framework for Systems of DPI', adopted under India's leadership of the G20, which outlines principles for designing and deploying DPIs, is expected to emerge as an indispensable tool as countries operationalize their DPI roadmaps. India has also committed to set up an accompanying knowledge platform—a virtual Global DPI Repository—to host DPI-focused tools, resources, practices and experiences from around the globe.[24] As the world inches towards 2030, the proven impact of DPI in terms of galvanizing inclusive development, seamless public service delivery, and the digital economy will become a fulcrum for advocacy.

[23]'India, US to develop, deploy digital public infra in developing countries', *The Economic Times*, 6 July 2023, https://tinyurl.com/y7ufu8xu. Accessed on 14 August 2024.

[24]'Digital Economy Ministers Meeting Outcome Document and Chair Summary', *G20*, 19 August 2023, https://tinyurl.com/5c2uazb2. Accessed on 10 February 2024.

There are indications that the climate of enthusiasm surrounding DPIs could infect the ongoing Brazilian G20 presidency too. According to President Lula, Brazil's tenure presents a 'unique opportunity for the sustainable development agenda',[25] and the 'fight against [...] extreme poverty and inequality' will be a driving priority.[26] These are challenges that DPIs have been able to tackle head-on in other parts of the world. Besides, Brazil has enjoyed much success with several of its own population-scale digital infrastructures; and some Brazilian stakeholders have expressed an interest in aligning its digital systems with the Indian DPI approach, or applying certain elements of India Stack to its domestic contexts.[27] Brazil's Pix, for example, is a near equivalent of India's UPI; the country's much-lauded open finance system is based on consent-based data sharing, akin to DEPA; and it has been argued that Consumidor, an online dispute resolution system launched by the Brazilian government, could achieve fuller potential as a DPI if it were to introduce open standards or application programming interfaces for value-added services.[28]

Going forward, India is likely to seek to understand more closely what different countries would like to do—and in some cases are already doing—in the DPI space, and to provide them the necessary assistance. India is well placed to do this, given its legacy of cooperation and knowledge-

---

[25]'What to expect from Brazil's G20 presidency', *Wilson Center*, 4 December 2023, https:// https://tinyurl.com/m5pruaxz. Accessed on 14 August 2024.

[26]'President Lula reinforces Brasil's priorities by assuming leadership of the G20', G20, 1 December 2023, https://tinyurl.com/5dj9eh98. Accessed on 14 August 2024.

[27]'Brazil's digital governance outperforms expectations: What can India learn?', *PropertyPistol*, 27 November 2023, https://tinyurl.com/49a77mz3. Accessed on 14 August 2024.

[28]'Accelerating the SDGs through Digital Public Infrastructure', UNDP.

sharing through MOSIP, and more recently through its MOUs with partner nations.

Finally, the future could witness a rise in global awareness about the link between DPIs and AI development efforts. Large volumes of data are a critical component of DPIs, and they could be an asset for training AI models, provided the principles of data privacy and security are firmly upheld. As part of DEPA 2.0, for instance, India is already experimenting with a solution called Confidential Clean Rooms, which are 'secure computing environments where sensitive data can be accessed in an algorithmically controlled manner for model training'.[29] As more countries begin to understand and implement these approaches, DPIs could help unleash a new wave of AI-based solutions.

---

[29]Sharma, Sharad, and Antara Vats, 'Ready for India's AI ambitions: We are now one step closer to having modern regulation for and of AI', *Financial Express*, 9 August 2023, https://tinyurl.com/36ye5h62. Accessed on 14 August 2024.

Amrita Narlikar

President and Professor, German Institute for Global and Area Studies

A Secure, Inclusive, and Sustainable Globalization: The Bharat Way

DESPITE HAVING GENERATED MANY GLOBAL BENEFITS (including poverty reduction), globalization has been under attack from the political left, right and populists of different types. Unfortunately, its ardent defenders—often well-meaning liberals—have not helped the cause. Caught between the doomsayers who warn against the dire consequences of deglobalization and denialists who argue that reports of discontent are greatly exaggerated, the political and intellectual space for a serious and much-needed reform of economic interdependence has narrowed. Globalization is undoubtedly worth preserving for the many gains that it brings to many people. But this, in turn, requires a fundamental reconsideration of both its direction and scale. In this essay, I present a brief overview of the problems inherent in the current model of globalization. In the second section, I explain why Bharat may be uniquely placed to lead the way towards a more secure, inclusive and sustainable globalization. The Raisina Dialogue can serve as the flagship for this for reasons that I outline in the third section. In the same section, I offer an agenda for future research and dialogue.

THE LIMITS OF GLOBALIZATION

The critique and questioning of globalization are far from new. But the discontent has grown over the last decade and entered the mainstream. In part, the backlash against globalization is a product of inadequate narratives on the part of the pro-globalizers. While the sceptics and critics have been vociferous and visible in advancing the anti-globalization story, the supporters of globalization have worked quietly under the assumption that globalization did not need 'selling' because its benefits should be obvious to all.[1]

The election of Donald J. Trump to the US presidency, with his 'America First' agenda, and the Brexit Referendum in 2016 provided powerful illustrations of the widespread appeal of an anti-globalization narrative. Importantly, this is not just an issue of 'communication' or framing. As the years have gone by, the content of globalization has also left much to be desired. Three deficits—involving security, sustainability and ownership—render the current model of globalization precarious.[2]

First, increasingly integrated global value chains, which form a core part of globalization today, have also created new security vulnerabilities that some states are better able to exploit and hold to ransom than others.[3] Second,

---

[1]Narlikar, Amrita, *Poverty Narratives and Power Paradoxes in International Trade Negotiations and Beyond*, Cambridge University Press, New York, 2020. Also see: Howse, Robert, 'From Politics to Technocracy and back again: The Fate of the Multilateral Trading System', *American Journal of International Law*, Vol. 96, No. 94 2002, pp. 94–117.

[2]Narlikar, Amrita, 'How Not to Negotiate: The Case of Trade Multilateralism', *International Affairs*, Vol. 98, No. 5, 2022, pp. 1553–1573, https://tinyurl.com/2tbetknc. Accessed on 14 August 2024.

[3]Farrell, Henry, and Abraham Newman, 'Weaponized Interdependence: How Global Economic Networks Shape State Coercion', *International Security*, Vol. 44, No. 1, 2019, pp. 42–79.

although globalization has contributed to the increasing prosperity and longevity of humans globally, this has come at horrific costs to other species that inhabit the planet. For instance, the World Wildlife Fund reports 'an average 69 per cent decline in the relative abundance of monitored wildlife populations around the world between 1970 and 2018'.[4] Factory farming, export of live animals, trade in animal parts, encroachment on wild lands and forests—all intrinsic parts of the globalization that many of us have known and cherished—have resulted in needless suffering and death, biodiversity loss, as well as adverse effects on human health (including pandemics). Third, despite repeated pronouncements in the West that the North–South divide is a thing of the past, large swathes of the 'Global South' have been united in their frustration with the international institutions that govern diverse aspects of globalization.[5] This discontent is evident within international organizations (ranging from the UN Security Council to the World Trade Organization, or WTO) as well as in the parallel institutions that have emerged (such as the expanded BRICS and the India-led Voice of the Global South Summit).

Fixing these problems will be a tall order, but it is clear that a business-as-usual approach will also not work. A balance between idealism and pragmatism is needed, together with

---

[4]WWF (2022), *Living Planet Report 2022 – Building a nature- positive society*, Almond, R.E.A., M. Grooten, D. Juffe Bignoli, and T. Petersen, eds., WWF, Gland, Switzerland, https://tinyurl.com/yeyvca22. Accessed on 14 August 2024.

[5]Kürzdörfer, Nora, and Amritia Narlikar, 'Was ist Schon ein Name', *Internationale Politik*, https://tinyurl.com/22mvap4n, 28 August 2023; republished in English as 'A Rose by Any Other Name? In Defence of the Global South', *Global Policy*, 29 August 2023, https://tinyurl.com/55vrwr3r. Accessed on 14 August 2024.

some out-of-the-box thinking. The India that is Bharat has much to offer in this regard.

THE BHARAT WAY?

Bharat has many strengths to draw on as a world leader to reshape globalization: its experience—even before its emergence as independent India—in negotiating the institutions of global order, long-standing democratic credentials and civilizational identity allow it to turn to ancient ideas that sometimes serve as a useful guide to tackle modern problems.[6] I offer three pathways that could form a part of a Bharatiya approach to globalization, which would begin to address the problems identified in the previous section.

A SECURE GLOBALIZATION

First, even at a time when the rest of the world was gung-ho about pushing for globalization, India maintained considerable caution. This was evident in its trade negotiations, both under the umbrella of the General Agreement on Tariffs and Trade (GATT) as well as the WTO. For the negotiation positions that it took, it encountered (sometimes bitter) critique. Today—although some of that critique still persists[7]—India is far from alone in its scepticism

---

[6]Narlikar, Aruna, Amitabh Mattoo, and Amrita Narlikar, *Strategic Choices, Ethical Dilemmas: Stories from the Mahabharat*, Penguin Random House, Delhi, 2023.

[7]For instance, 'In a predictable pantomime that precedes WTO Ministerial Conferences, some countries are positioning themselves as obstacles to consensus... For India, this is old hat. The Indians held up consensus—a key principle that underpins and increasingly hamstrings decision-making at the WTO—at Ministerial Conferences in 2001, 2013, and 2015. Its

about over-reliance on global markets. While its emphasis on food security and the issue of public stockholding continue to encounter resistance in the WTO, its own emphasis on manufacturing via Atmanirbhar Bharat has parallels in the industrial policies of developed countries. What was an anachronistic opposition to trade liberalization in the 2000s now looks like far-sighted leadership in a world of weaponized interdependence.[8]

India's deeply ingrained policy mindset that recognizes the trade-offs between trade and security is precisely what the institutions of global economic governance need if the rules underpinning globalization are to be made fit for purpose again.

AN INCLUSIVE GLOBALIZATION

Second, in terms of creating greater ownership of the process of reforming globalization, India occupies a special position. As a democracy, it has vital links with the liberal West; as a key player concerned about the imbalance of power in the Indo–Pacific, it plays an important role as a Quad member; as a rising power seeking reform, it cooperates with the original and expanded BRICS. Just as importantly, while cooperating with the incumbent and rising powers, its commitment to other developing countries has only increased. This is quite a different role from the one played by its neighbour China. And it is a role that Bharat has embraced not only for its

---

record in other free trade agreements is similar.' See Rockwell, Keith, 'A Moment of Truth for the WTO', *Hinrich Foundation*, Singapore, 6 February 2024. https://tinyurl.com/589nvr65. Accessed on 14 August 2024.

[8]I made this argument in Narlikar, Amrita, 'India's Foreign Economic Policy under Modi: Negotiations and Narratives in the WTO and beyond', *International Politics*, Vol. 59, (2021 online, 2022 in print), pp. 148–156, https://tinyurl.com/2dfbw2sw. Accessed on 14 August 2024.

own advantage but for the global good too.

The country's impressive leadership of the G20 presidency (which also saw the transformation of the G20 into the G21, with the African Union becoming a full member of the group) provides an example of Bharat's successful consensus-building abilities and inclusive approach. This inclusiveness was also illustrated in the cross-country involvement of peoples, with ministerials and meetings taking place in different cities of its large geography. Just as important were the dynamic and lively outreach processes of India's G20 presidency, which brought together diverse constituencies. The self-confident Bharat that we see in action knows how to build bridges across squabbling giants while ensuring that the interests of smaller players are represented and voiced.

A SUSTAINABLE AND KINDER GLOBALIZATION

Third, and perhaps the most important of Bharat's contributions, is the concept and pursuit of a planet-centric globalization. In this regard, much is made of India's G20 theme—*Vasudhaiva Kutumbakam*: 'One Earth, One Family, One Future'—which many interpret to refer to the global family of nations and peoples. In fact, however, the concept is more inclusive than that: it refers to not only our human kin but also the other beings that form a part of the global policy, with whom we share this planet. Across the epics of the Mahabharata and the Ramayana, and through verses in a variety of ancient texts that form a part of India's lived traditions, resonates the idea आत्मवत् सर्वभूतेषु, यः पष्यति सः पण्डितः ('he who looks upon all beings as he looks upon himself, he is the truly wise one'). Individual beings and entire species who have no vote and no voice count as much in this Bharatiya idea of a global family, as human beings and humankind.[9] Incorporate this idea into an updated model of globalization, and we finally have a chance of making globalization genuinely sustainable and equitable.

RAISINA DIALOGUE

As it enters its tenth year and the next decade, the space that the Raisina Dialogue creates for independent thinking and frank exchange will be more important than ever. India, its host country, will have a key role to play in shaping globalization. As a self-reflecting leader, Bharat will be well-served to lead by example. It will be able to lead with confidence and credibility, developing and applying the tenets highlighted in the previous section not only on the global stage but also domestically and in cooperation with like-minded partners. This creates new avenues for research and debate on geoeconomics (in areas ranging from food security to industrial policy and digital technologies to defence), global governance, and ethics in statecraft.

The Raisina Dialogue itself (and its related publications, such as *Raisina Files* and *Raisina Debates*) has been highly cognizant of the risks inherent in globalization. Authors and speakers have been alerting the world to the dangers of a naïve over-reliance on economic interdependence, and they have also been asking for likeminded partners to deepen trade linkages. They have recognized the importance of interests and have also not shied away from addressing

---

[9]Narlikar, Amrita, 'The Ancient Roots of Global Bharat', in Pant, Harsh, and Sameer Patil, eds., *The Making of a Global Bharat*, ORF-Global Policy Special Issue, February 2024; Narlikar, Amrita, '"One Earth, One Family, One Future": Unpacking the Theme of G20's India Presidency and its Wide-Ranging Implications', in Chaturvedi, Sachin, and Sabyasachi Saha, eds., *Well-Being, Values, and Lifestyles – Towards a New Development Paradigm*, Springer, Berlin, 2025; Narlikar et al., 2023.

testy questions of values.[10] Indulging in neither alarmism nor complacency, the Dialogue's multimedia and multistakeholder engagement constitutes a serious commitment to facilitating fearless thinking and finding constructive solutions.

In contrast to the Munich Security Conference and the World Economic Forum, the Raisina Dialogue stands out for its location in a democratic nation in the Global South. It is more inclusive and more diverse: its outreach processes enable the participation of the interested public, in contrast to the closed-door meetings that take place behind security cordons in Munich and Davos. While ensuring a diversity of voices—even those that are sometimes 'cancelled' on Western platforms—is represented on its forums, participants do not accept lowest common denominator solutions. Authors and speakers are ready to draw clear red lines when needed.[11]

There is an edginess here—of the good and healthy kind.

---

[10]e.g. Narlikar, Amrita, 'Emerging Narratives and the Future of Multilateralism', in Saran, Samir and Preeti Lourdes, eds., *Raisina Files*, 2021, https://tinyurl.com/t3ysr2xt; Narlikar, Amrita, 'Scripting a Third Way: The Importance of EU-India Partnership', *Raisina Debates*, 14 August 2023, https://tinyurl.com/5h65a47v; Narlikar, Amrita, and Samir Saran, 'All Roads Connect Delhi and Brussels', *Raisina Debates*, 24 April 2022, https://tinyurl.com/mm4e9fyd. Accessed on 14 August 2024.

[11]e.g. The outbreak of the pandemic in 2020, when most were pussyfooting around the role of the World Health Organization, the creator and curator of Raisina Dialogue courageously wrote a scathing and timely article: Saran, Samar, '#COVID19: Dr WHO Gets Prescription Wrong', *Health Express*, 25 March 2020, https://tinyurl.com/4pxvam59; another critical piece which generated timely public debate was: Narlikar, Amrita, and Samir Saran, 'The European Union, CAI and the Abyss', *Raisina Debates*, 2 January 2021, https://tinyurl.com/4d4jmytu. Accessed on 14 August 2024.

Marcelo Ebrard

Minister of Economy of Mexico

Connecting Worlds: India's Role as a 'Bridge-Builder'

DURING MY ALMOST FIVE-YEAR TENURE AS THE FOREIGN Minister of Mexico, the search for closer relations with the Asia–Pacific region was amongst my top priorities. The growing importance of the Asia–Pacific region is indisputable, highlighted by its commitment to multilateralism and open trade. We are talking about a region that comprises more than 60 per cent of the world's population, over 40 per cent of global trade, and more than 40 per cent of worldwide GDP.

Within the Asia–Pacific region, India is a key player with whom Mexico has had diplomatic relations for over 70 years. In recent times, relations between our two nations have strengthened and flourished. India stands as Mexico's tenth largest trading partner with further prospects to expand bilateral economic cooperation and harness synergies between our two emerging economies. We also have a growing trade and economic complementarity, as well as thriving cooperation in diverse fields. There is potential to explore and collaborate in the sectors of aerospace, health, joint pharmaceutical manufacturing, space exploration, agriculture and renewables—areas where India is a global leader— and boost our privileged partnership to a strategic one. Simultaneously, both India and Mexico endeavour towards a common vision of a stable multipolar world order. Our countries have succeeded in establishing a fluent political dialogue, identifying areas of agreement and joint initiatives in the multilateral arena.

BUILDING A BOND

Our relationship has been characterized by a spate of diplomatic exchanges in recent years that have provided ongoing momentum. Among the official trips I made to countries in the region as Foreign Minister, I wish to underline my two visits to India, in April 2022 and March 2023. Furthermore, Indian External Affairs Minister S. Jaishankar visited Mexico in September 2021. With my Indian counterpart, we agreed on a common vision for the future of our bilateral relations. These high-level meetings, along with productive and fruitful interactions between Mexican and Indian delegations from different government agencies, have been of utmost importance in strengthening our bilateral relations.

A significant step forward in our efforts to foster links between Mexico and India was the opening of a new Mexican Consulate in Mumbai in 2023. Significantly, during my last trip to India in March 2023, I had the honour of speaking at the 2023 edition of the Raisina Dialogue.

The Raisina Dialogue is considered by world leaders and academics in the Asia–Pacific region and beyond as one of the top platforms for the exchange of high-level ideas on current affairs. In line with India's growing influence in the world, this forum has become a flagship conference on geopolitics and geoeconomics.

The 2023 edition of the Raisina Dialogue was orchestrated timely, as it was held immediately after the meeting of foreign ministers of the G20, chaired by India. This allowed both speakers and attendees to have a fruitful and enriching experience in assessing current world affairs. In that fortunate coincidence, I was able to share some ideas and thoughts in the session titled 'The New High-Table: Realigning the G20 in a Changing World', related to the G20 and Mexico's value-added participation in this venue. The session was particularly relevant, considering that in 2023 India held the presidency of the G20. I had the opportunity to underline the Mexican conviction that the multilateral system should be protected and strengthened. The G20 is a strategic platform to advance this purpose and positively contribute to global governance.

India presided over the G20 presidency in challenging times for the global economy, deeply compromised by the effects of a global pandemic, and a war that endangered food supplies and created the deepest energy crisis since the 1970s.

Mexico fully supported India's G20 presidency and worked closely with all the other member states to ensure that the New Delhi Summit delivered positive results. Mexico will continue building on the role of the G20 as a platform for dialogue and consensus.

DIALOGUE AND DEPENDABILITY

It is worrying that geopolitical confrontations are becoming a growing barrier to compromise on the most pressing global crises, amidst at least two conflicting visions of global governance. Simultaneously, we are seeing a period of four emerging economies presiding over the G20—Indonesia (2022), India (2023), Brazil (2024) and South Africa (2025)—and this is undoubtedly an opportunity to increase the influence of the developing world in the formulation of the grouping's agenda.

In this context, the Raisina Dialogue last year, coinciding with India's G20 presidency, placed emphasis on the Global South and the problems and priorities for this disparate group of countries: it raised the voice of developing nations by retaining the focus on development issues such as climate change, poverty, debt crises, and sustainable development. This is crucial because the active involvement of emerging countries contributes to the provision of global public goods and supports the integration of low-income and developing countries—those suffering the worst impacts of global crises—into a sustainable global economy. Thus, the Raisina Dialogue has evolved into a platform for a strategic dialogue on key social, security, environmental and financial challenges, as well as being an agenda setter and facilitator.

At the same time, during its G20 presidency, India positioned itself as a bridge between the developed and developing worlds. The diverse panels, in terms of themes, composition and widespread representation, at the Raisina Dialogue 2023 recognized emerging economies such as India and Mexico as bridge-builders in their own regions, with growing influence in a context defined by bloc formation and geopolitical competition.

In today's polarized world, it is more imperative than ever that dialogue, cooperation and solidarity drive our aspirations. Stability, peace and prosperity depend upon diplomacy and dialogue. Bringing together the world's decision-makers, policymakers and thought leaders under one roof, the Raisina Dialogue is an embodiment of this spirit of dialogue and dissent. Mexico, too, advocates for the use of dialogue and the peaceful settlement of international disputes in any conflict.

The Raisina Dialogue also attempts to include voices that have been historically overlooked within discussions and policy formulation processes. These include the voices of women, youth and migrants, giving particular attention to gender equality and the protection of human rights as cross-cutting issues. The Raisina Young Fellows Programme is a testament to this endeavour of inclusion. After all, addressing global challenges requires inclusion and dialogue, not exclusion and isolation. In this scenario, the Raisina Dialogue plays a constructive role in promoting dialogue and contributing to lasting solutions for present and future global challenges.

I am deeply grateful and honoured to be the first Mexican Minister of Foreign Affairs to participate in the Raisina Dialogue.

On the eve of completing its first decade, the Raisina Dialogue has become a reference in addressing the most challenging issues that the international community faces. In the G20 as well as in Raisina Dialogue and other fora, Mexico will keep underlining its firm commitment to the protection and strengthening of the multilateral system.

My special gratitude to the Minister of External Affairs of India, Dr S. Jaishankar, and the President of the Observer Research Foundation, Dr Samir Saran, for inviting me to share Mexico's vision in these complex times.

Stephen J. Harper

Former Prime Minister of Canada

India Takes Its Rightful Place in an Evolving Global Order

INDIA'S EMERGENCE HAS CONSEQUENCES NOT ONLY FOR its 1.4 billion population but for the world as a whole. From the stability of the Indo–Pacific region and the health of global democracy to implementing the Sustainable Development Goals (SDGs) and tackling climate change, success in addressing every contemporary issue today is contingent to a significant degree on India's actions. Its choices will have a profound impact in shaping much of humanity's future and the world's trends.

In this context, India's rise is rightly perceived as largely a force for good. In a world of competing visions and deep divides, India represents that much-needed bridge and meeting point while also generally sitting on the right side of important questions of values.

It is my belief that the world is dividing into two significant blocs, American-led and Chinese-led, in what is effectively a Cold War 2.0. That said, many players do not wish to simply slot into these two blocs. In the case of India, sheer size and the growing strength of the economy render a more independent position possible.

From my (Western) perspective, this is not a bad thing. The weakness of Western leadership, especially its contradictory penchants for nihilistic self-censure and haughty moral hectoring, is paving the way for an alternative democratic voice. India, by contrast, is buzzing with optimism and ambition. The country is modernizing and moving forward at home while also forging a myriad of new global partnerships that represent a new kind of globalization.

For example, India's push, during its G20 presidency, to ensure the development agenda does not fall off the global high table has garnered widespread international support. India has spoken not merely for itself but for an entire cohort of nations from Africa to Latin America and others by putting forward their concerns. The same can be said for India's contribution to other global debates, ranging from climate change and geopolitical conflict to the reform of multilateral institutions. This is forcing many in the West to sit up and listen to views from the vast Global South.

THE GLOBAL NEED

The twenty-first century is often touted as the Asian Century. But the vast Asian continent is no monolith, and the rise of different Asian powers has starkly different implications for international security, rules-based multilateralism and the global economy. Which set of values gain dominance and ultimately prevail will determine whether the global system is characterized by coercion and disruption or by cooperation and collaboration.

A few years ago, I expressed my view at the Raisina Dialogue that India's democracy would not become a mere echo of Western liberalism, but would be shaped by its own culture and its own nationalism. Some years later, at the Raisina Dialogue in 2022, EAM S. Jaishankar espoused a similar view when he emphasized that India should engage the world with confidence based on its identity, rather than attempt to please the world by becoming a pale imitation of others. And this, I think we can all agree, is happening. India is taking its rightful place in an evolving global order—in line with its own traditions—and carving out its own path.

Today, under Prime Minister Narendra Modi, India stands virtually alone as a democracy with both strong leadership and a forward direction. The pilgrimages of the world's diplomats to New Delhi and global businesspeople all over India are a testament to that fact. While the West seems to be in retreat, India is deftly creating linkages and navigating the pushes and pulls of a complex international arena. Its beliefs in both itself and an interconnected world lie behind the depth and diversity of India's seemingly contradictory partnerships—from north to south, east to west.

This is a challenging period, particularly for democracies and heterogeneous societies generally. While one war nears its third year, another breaks out, polarizing communities and nations worldwide. The war in Ukraine, the conflict in the Middle East, and China's destabilizing tactics in its neighbourhood serve as critical reminders that stability cannot be taken for granted and that greater deterrence, partnership and cooperation are required.

These conflicts are fought not just in the field of battle but also through the battle of values and ideas. The modern digital space is one of both immense opportunities and serious threats, linking security challenges in one part of the world with those elsewhere. Economic interdependence can also be weaponized. These complex new-age challenges are being accompanied by strife and struggle for basics like food and energy. To deal with this volatility, but also to seize the possibilities, we need sane voices to rise over the din.

It is in times like these that the circulation of people, ideas and viewpoints, often contrary and opposed, is even more important. The Raisina Dialogue, with its wide-ranging and far-reaching deliberations, has emerged as a successful effort to discuss the substantive issues of our time. Entering the tenth year of its inception, Raisina is an extrapolation of India's ambitions and its global positioning. As a hub for some of the most consequential global conversations taking place during a period of intense transition, it epitomizes India's newfound confidence and assuredness.

This forum, which has grown dramatically year on year, is conspicuous in its efforts to feature the voices of traditionally under-represented constituencies. It is not just another bastion of entitled elites but one genuinely reflective of the world's ethnic, gender and ideological diversity. Special attention is paid to the next generation through initiatives like the Raisina Young Fellows Programme. Raisina does this because, for conversations to be impactful, the voices of our future need to be heard.

I have had the honour of expressing my views at the Raisina Dialogue several times since its inception in 2016. Evolving from India's flagship conference on geopolitics and geoeconomics to one of the world's most important forums, the Raisina Dialogue has come a long way. It brings together heads of state and government, thought leaders, policymakers, academia, and the business community each year in New Delhi under one roof. The Dialogue is, in short, a clear signal that India has shed its historical hesitations and is ready to play a proactive role in shaping global dynamics.

The world needs constructive and open dialogue, but also dialogue that is grounded in sound expertise and experience. Raisina, with its spirit of debate, dissent, deliberation, dissemination and diplomacy, provides just that.

I hope to continue being part of the Dialogue for many years to come.

David Petraeus

Former Director, Central Intelligence Agency

The Raisina Dialogue:
A Metaphor for India

THE RAISINA DIALOGUE HAS EMERGED AS A METAPHOR for India's rise. Drawing its name from the high ground in New Delhi on which the seat of the Indian government is located, the annual gathering has grown dramatically in size and significance over the past eight years, just as India itself has over that same period.

Having participated in Raisina in person over a number of years, as well as virtually during the COVID-19 pandemic, I have been privileged to watch it—and India—evolve first-hand during that period. Starting from the Dialogue's inception in 2016 with a regional focus, barely 100 speakers, and some 600 attendees, the gathering has grown in recent years to attract more than 2,600 attendees and speakers from 100 countries. In so doing, it has become a magnet for policymakers, business leaders, scholars, military commanders and students from all over the world. During that same time, India has seen similar growth and achieved comparably greater global prominence as well.

THE RAISINA ROAD

Raisina has thus mirrored—and promoted and benefitted from—India's evolution on the world stage from self-described 'diffidence' to 'confidence'. That is, in fact, the way Indian leaders explain the country's shift from deference on various global issues to increasing assertiveness on them. To be sure, this has been accompanied by the recognition that India needs to avoid 'over-confidence' even as it has become the fastest-growing large economy in the world, surpassed China as the largest country in the world, surpassed the UK to become the fifth-largest economy in the world, become increasingly significant diplomatically, and, in 2023 alone, hosted the G20, the Trilateral Commission, and the ICC Cricket World Cup.

These are, in short, heady times in India, and rightly so. And the rise of the Raisina Dialogue has accompanied India's dramatic increase in global importance. Indeed, again, the development of each has reinforced that of the other. As India has demonstrated increased leadership and influence in the world, the Raisina Dialogue has taken on ever greater prominence as well.

In its 2023 edition, Raisina provided a particularly striking reflection of India's vastly more prominent place in the world, offering further evidence that 'India has arrived' on the world stage in a way not seen before. Indeed, that assessment featured prominently in news accounts of the 2023 gathering, most notably with photos of the panel of foreign ministers of the countries that comprise the Quad (the US, Japan, Australia and India). They were joined at Raisina by numerous other serving and former heads of government, foreign ministers, military commanders, scholars, intelligence leaders and media personalities from all over the world who populated the 100 panels on the myriad subjects that were discussed.

Needless to say, India's occasionally unique—and some might say a bit ambiguous—role in the world has also featured on the stage at Raisina. In 2016, for example, in response to a suggestion I made to the then Foreign Secretary S. Jaishankar that it was time for India to choose a side in the world, he replied, 'We have chosen. We have taken India's side.' This captured the emerging reality succinctly and forthrightly, and, not surprisingly, it continues to explain India's stance on issues, as Jaishankar now serves as India's Minister of External Affairs and appears each year to address the Raisina Dialogue.

This reality has meant that even as India has embraced more fully its membership in the Quad, celebrated increased American investment in India, enjoyed record trade with the US, and broadly embraced democratic values and the rule of law, it has also kept a foot in the BRICS, bought increasing amounts of oil (albeit at a discount) from Russia despite Russia's invasion of Ukraine, and increasingly sought to include and represent the Global South in various multilateral fora. All of this has been on display and discussed at Raisina. And it is these dynamics that are shaping India's new identity in the world, with some elements that are applauded vigorously by the US and the West, and others that are embraced by the BRICS and the 'rest', with India seeking to ensure that the voices of the Global South and the dynamic described as the 'rise of the rest' are not lost on the leaders of the 'West'.

In sum, the rise of the Raisina Dialogue, now rivalling the Munich Security Forum and the Shangri-La Dialogue as a 'must-do' gathering, has both presaged and mirrored India's growth in prominence. Raisina has also benefitted from India's continued rise and, in various respects, contributed to it as well. Beyond that, it has helped capture and reflect the unique place in the world that India has been carving for itself. In so doing, Raisina has become a truly stimulating, informative, enjoyable and consequential gathering, and I look forward to returning to it for many years to come.